MW00686010

JUNK PERCUSSION

NOTES FOR THE FUTURE

ROGER TURNER

MARI KAMADA

© 2022 Roger Turner and Mari Kamada
All rights reserved.
ISBN 978-1-949597-32-5

Publisher: David Rothenberg
Editor and Designer: Colette McCormick
Set in Avenir

Terra Nova Editions

Terra Nova Press comes out of Cold Spring, New York and was
founded in 2019 to publish books on music, culture, and nature. Our
fast-track line is represented by the *Editions* collection.
.

www.terranovapress.com

JUNK PERCUSSION

PREFACE

This book presents a collection of writings about a series of photos taken of various, mainly found, percussion instruments belonging to me, that were once not musical instruments at all.

At a time when the need to document and assert identity has become a kind of international psycho-crisis, Mari Kamada and I have tried to show a side to documentation that can express a different creative energy and can slot into the cultural maelstrom in other ways. Not exactly a catalogue then, but tending towards a group of essays and photos that lean together.

I am extremely grateful therefore to Mari for her ability to intuit how best to conjure a visual life from these often damningly crude objects. Her extraordinary knowledge and perceptions of both music and the visual arts have helped resuscitate bits of metal and plastic, persuading them accordingly to vibrate on the page.

And so we set the material up, got the art-eyes primed, and took a lot of photos.

Initially, many of these instruments were objects that had once been discarded and later found by myself. Because I have been

JUNK

working as a drummer and percussionist for something like 50 years running around much of the world, I have collected some amazing things, some of which I am lucky enough to also have been given.

A couple of things have been physically adapted—certain cymbals re-shaped for example—but most are as they arrived. And, I must confess, quite a lot have been edited out and discarded, having sat long-enough unused in the boxes and bins of my drum room, gathering dust and feelings of neglect, and reminding me of Carl Andre's plaintive statement:

> The open end of my work is scavenging; just walking through the streets of the city, and coming upon construction sites, and finding groups of material and taking them. And often I have these groups sitting on the floor and I try to figure out what is the combination of these pieces, and sometimes it just doesn't happen and I get rid of them again.[1]

Yet there felt a kind of inevitability about this project, so it's not really coincidental at all that this has happened: musical instruments, we could surmise, have always been beautiful to the eye. But to focus specifically on an arena almost of chance, of the discarded or re-interpreted—the hitherto un-focused-on scraps and detritus—gives the exercise perhaps an edge that carries its musical centre into a world also inhabited by art.

But whatever we may consider or conclude, one of the qualities Mari and I have tried to express in some of the photos is less about simply rhapsodizing their subjects, but more about indicating the magic of transporting them into the realms of truly being musical instruments.

Mari's creative focus has allowed this documentation to suggest the energies that a piece of scrap metal can occasionally offer to the music world, giving it a space to also proclaim a certain beauty. All musicians and lovers of visual arts can surely appreciate that.

Does junk ever exist? Junk abounds? Does the drummer abide?

This short book might in many ways be considered a homage to the musically unexpected. It could also be viewed as an appreciation of a logical progression in acoustic music languages, one that recognises that these vocabularies can integrate the past with the contemporary emphasis on electronic, even computer-based, and certainly electro-acoustic musics.

As we should discover, "junk, or "non-manufactured"percussion, indeed has a legacy, both in the music world and by extension also in the visual arts. With music, perhaps the names Varese or John Cage can jump most readily to mind, to some extent offering a core validity to this aspect of music investigation. In art vocabularies, the use of junk, found objects, garbage, industrial or other materials, together with the conceptual positioning of numerous artists and art groups, has long been respected. Duchamp's "Fountain" stuck a urinal in front of the public's gaze in 1917; Dada used all manner of found objects in sculptural and wall imaging; Rauschenberg offered an extraordinary range of objects and materials, from industrial metal detritus to cardboard boxes and cloth; and the Japanese Gutai Art Association of 1954 and the later Fluxus movement were insistent both on experimenting with materials hitherto outside the consensus for art use and, placing great importance on situational performativity, on experimenting with how those materials would be used. For Gutai, crucially, the process rather than the product seemed to be the essential thing, a concept that also relates very much to certain thinking found in international music improvisation positioning.

That the visual arts have long been allowed to carry a wide range of exploratory vocabularies whilst, in terms of public acceptance, the music world has been relatively confined, has been a cause for never-ending debate. That language perhaps controls perception and presents an argument that forces the discussion: are we allowed to include musical languages, and what then when perception is allowed to contain the auditory?

The term "percussion"—much like the term "music" itself—can accommodate all kinds of material, and we might realise that once we've opened our ears to the timbres of "junk" instruments, they cease to be "junk" at all and simply start belonging to the world of instruments we all know, standing very much in line with certain approaches to how we think about sound and, indeed, music. "Junk" becomes simply a term of convenience.

This book then addresses issues about "outsider" acoustic percussion, found objects, the stuff not stocked by nor bought in shops. The photographs show these objects in a way that grants them their status as musical "instruments," allowing them expression and identity. This is important, because we are also intent on talking about these percussion items less as decorative add-ons to what may be considered the main musical material, and more as instruments to be integrated into a music's design. This can be recognised in the way that drums and percussion may be phrased and played in improvisation and certain contemporary compositions, not only for their variety of timbres and tones, but also for what they can provide to even a broadly "melodic," line-playing design to music-making, also at fast tempos. I suppose I am thinking primarily of the multidimensional possibilities of free improvisation, a kind of rhizomatic approach to music-making.

However, as a background perspective supporting this liberalisation and elevation of percussion, we might keep in mind Reed and Leach's observation about the direction a mix of percussion with "accepted and defined" instruments can attain in this regard, and that this book addresses. They stated that:

> The instruments of indefinite pitch can usually only simulate pitch contour; but [they] have an uncanny way of absorbing pitches when doubled with instruments of definite pitch. They seem to be definite-pitched... The awareness of these pitch differences makes it possible to write melodically for the indefinite-pitched percussion instruments.[2]

Some might say the drummer-percussionist plays the instruments closest to the heart of improvisation. The drumset seems a less defined instrument than, say, the trumpet, even, an instrument that in fact does have its own variations of form. Today, the drummer-percussionist is able to engage with the material of the set in personal ways, not simply in the technique they adapt and adopt, but by the choices of instrumentation they make. When we look at the equipment of simply contemporary drumset drummers, we see differences in the materials the drums are made from: are they maple, African mahogany, birch, beech, oak etc., made with plies or one-piece shells, or made from acrylics, copper, brass? Then there's the size of the drums, the number of the drums, the ways they are grouped together, how they are tuned, which kind of drumheads they have, the size and number of cymbals, the alloy the cymbals are made from, where they are placed, cymbals with holes in, cymbals with rivets in, and cymbals with stands sometimes so heavy they guarantee a hernia for whoever carries and sets them up.

Indeed, setting up drums and percussion lends itself to a certain fluidity of change within its own nature. It is less defined and constricted than most other instruments, and of itself approaches the spirit of improvisation openly and readily. Look at the drumsets of the early jazz musicians—some with home-made frames, with the percussion suspended. That percussion could even be kitchen pots and pans, something Charles "Buddy" Gilmore touched on in his intricate percussion set-up in the 1910s. Cage's 1959 "Water Walk," with its use of domestic appliances and a bath full of water, was really extending a percussive tradition. Indeed, who would have thought that even bells for cows would be welcomed so totally into the industry of contemporary music?

The variety and source of the sounds these kinds of equipment-units employ have evolved through the demands and practicalities of the music their use helped create, and of course by the person doing the playing. Naturally enough, they can change according to taste and choice, but we cannot underestimate the nature of the equipment demanded for many works involving percussion in contemporary "classical" composition. Instruments from "outside the family" abound: bottles in Brian Ferneyhough's "Bone Alphabet," for example; magazines, cardboard, books, etc., in John Cage's "Living Room Music," and enormous amounts of equipment for his "Third Construction." It could be a long list.

For the contemporary player or composer intent on exploring and opening vocabularies, this all offers an endless variety of possibilities: instruments from western culture as well as everywhere else, and not only from the manufacturers who fill the drum shops, but from the neighbourhood where material gets discarded, and where expanding ecologies provide ideas and fresh musical possibilities. The drummer or percussionist fully engaged in researching textures and pitches and sound spectrums has the freedom to choose instruments in ways that the violinist perhaps cannot, unless the violinist chooses to liberate the instrument from its standard form to—what?—perhaps a carefully adapted disposable polystyrene body, or a plank of wood, a tube of aluminium. Would it then be a violin, so defined is the instrument historically, in our ears and minds?

Drums, and maybe even percussion, are also of course defined in the minds of Western listeners, despite the information glut that arrived with the internet. But maybe their size is not, nor shape or construction; and certainly, neither is that enormous possibility of variables grouped under that extraordinary category: "percussion." Who said it: "everything has a sound"? The only problem there is first to be aware of how these sounds behave and how they can be played, and then find the music that can accommodate those instruments and allow those sounds to be made. Then, of course, the major issue arrives: can you get them to the concert?

We usually think of getting our musical instruments in prescribed shops, or at least through sources that deal in "instruments" as defined items with components and forms—identities—that can be manufactured. We usually want a sound that is similarly repeatable and defined by the standards of known and approved music. The saxophone and the mouthpiece and the reed that gets us a little towards sounding like Lester Young, or indeed the snare drum that might help propel the Art Blakey crush roll.

But if we are looking for a sound vocabulary for a different music, one that in itself is less defined in the public's ear, maybe less willing to be commodified, what then?

The shop, with its polished goods on display and with their perhaps equally polished sounds offering even more allure, might not offer instruments that fit the bill or might only fit it partially. And, of course, these might cost you more than you want to pay or might give you a vocabulary covered by endless others across the planet— nothing particularly appropriate to your culture or your environment, or, in fact, to you.

Well, in that case, the percussionists among us are able to look elsewhere, and assemble a group of instruments of a different kind, looking and sounding... different. And what's more, being on the lookout, they can pick these up in all kinds of locations, and make life a much more interesting affair than just calling into over-priced shops, familiar to all or listed in online tourist guides. And if you follow this less mapped course of interest and action, you can adapt what you then have according to your needs, who you are playing with, or even what you can manage to carry. And so—of course— you can figure out for yourself how exactly you're going to play it, where and when you're going to use it. Very enjoyable, yet also fundamentally totally serious.

With a collection of "found" objects, a fluid vocabulary can be adopted, and the qualities of this can inspire and influence how one approaches playing the standard, "accepted" instruments.

It was so good to find that Man Ray had a series of works termed "objects of my affection." Percussionists can really relate to that.

Leedy Drum Topics was a newspaper published by the Leedy Drum Company of Indianapolis, U.S.A. from 1923 to 1941, and primarily put together by their sales' manager George H. Way. By issue 9 they were printing 50,000 copies, though later, because of expense, there were only between 2 to 4 issues produced per year.

Nevertheless, the *Leedy Drum Topics* publications were full of ideas for percussive effects sent in by readers and approved of by the Leedy editorial board. We get, for example, in the January 1931 edition, an airplane effect using a "cheap massage machine such as may be procured in any drug store." Moving "the vibrator" across the head of a "tympano" using "more or less pressure according to the effect desired" produced the desired sound… Or in the March 1932 edition: dragging the Leedy rumble tip across a fibre snare drum case propped against a chair leg gives an effect "something like a bass fiddle but of a new quality of sound." Or again we have an "emergency homemade locomotive effect" involving four tin cans and a spring.[3]

These ideas are great for sound-effects and were vital for the silent film era, but transferring those sounds into music-making is the thing. A context needs to be forged for this to be made possible. It's one of many reasons why improvisation as an approach to creating music carries such a relevant energy. It allows vocabularies to be extended and certain pertinent musical ideas to live. For the drummer-percussionist this is a crucial factor, giving value to experimentation and fresh expression that they might otherwise just not arrive at.

But, having said all this, musical experiments and investigations crop up in the most unexpected environments. Let's not forget, though I suspect we easily could, that even the U.S. army these days seems to have its musical antennae primed. When discussing the implements used to strike suspended cymbals, the training circular provided by the July 2018 Headquarters of the Department of the Army, Washington, DC, states:

> With a little experimenting, many interesting and imaginative sounds can be produced on suspended cymbals. Your prime concern should be musical taste while preventing damage to the cymbal. Brushes produce a light, airy effect only heard in soft passages. For louder passages, you can use a specially made heavy, stiff wire brush. Bass violin bows produce a screeching effect when the cymbal edge is bowed like a violin. Triangle beaters, coat hangers, bass guitar strings, coins, and chains all produce a variety of scraping or sizzling effects when drawn against the grain of the rings. Be careful not to damage the tone ring.4

All this caring, creative flair from the U.S. Army! Well, knock me over with an L85A2 assault rifle. Who would have thought it? ("'Assault' rifle?" questions the editor. I mean, of course, not that other sort of rifle armies use, the friendly one that sprays warm custard towards the opposition.)

And just in case we thought they were joking, we are told that for triangle there are several implements useable for special effects, including a spike or large nail, knitting needles of various sizes, and wooden coat hanger rods. Interestingly, they also remind us that "because each triangle has its own musical personality, every player must experiment with the triangle to locate its different playing areas. A triangle has more than 10 playing areas, each one sounding differently."5 The Washington army music instructor talks about the use of chains and brake drum cylinders, anvils, thunder sheets…you name it, the army's on it. So, the next time we see a regiment marching onwards, all bayonets and helmets, we know in their spare time many of them will be rubbing a triangle with a knitting needle, possibly making music together to fend off the deprivations of the world outside. Is this the setting for the birth of a new avant-garde blues? Despite the uniformity we vaguely hear about with armies, the individual struggles on under a "long live the triangle" banner, the much lauded and reborn instrument of freedom. And why not? What does it take to make an epiphany happen? Can the concept of what an "army" is be transformed? And maybe music will re-vitalise the planet after all.

(But no, of course it won't. Too many leaks. And for sure, neither will an army.)

The issue here, however, is that the use of percussion—the playing of percussion—has long been a liberating factor in socio-musical life. We may be forgiven for thinking it the vehicle for or signpost of liberation in many cultures, even today. Drum circles, samba bands, children's skills and development, and everyone tapping their feet to a song. Perhaps there is another truth shining through here: that one can indeed apply the creative imagination to percussion in ways one may never quite get to playing an oboe. Its form is less fixed, the techniques for playing it may be less stringently defined, it is less formidable, it's user-friendly, and it's fun. (I have been reminded, however, that playing the oboe has been known to even transcend these obstacles, a factor that Garvin Bushell would have touched on, no doubt, in Coltrane's group at the Village Vanguard in 1961.)

But ultimately, who really knows and who dictates the balance of power within such issues? The politics/economics of instrument accessibility? Cultural tropes? Additionally, however, and as implied above, playing percussion can be a group thing. The first instruments, voice and percussion: groups, communities, social activity things. By 1983, the musicologist and professor, Philip Tagg, tells us the Ewe people of south-east Ghana had still found no place for the western concept of "music" within their own cultural experience and language. The nearest equivalent seemed to be "vu ha," where "vu" means "drum" and "ha" means song.[6] As Mr. Cage reminded us: if the term music offends, *don't use it.*

Yet one's cultural environment is ever-shifting. As Tagg continued to point out: "the Ewe people use the English term 'music' to denote musical situations and structures imported by British colonialism and Anglo-American neo-colonialism." A good thing some people on the planet have some sense. "Music," it seems, can be culturally invasive, and it can steal qualities from peoples and sell them.

"Environment," as we might recognise today with a certain perplexity, has become a large, ever-expanding word, and we might assume that as a part of and a reflection of environment even in the west— as everything else is—percussion itself becomes a cultural factor that also expands—or perversely, indeed contracts—with you. In general, it defines itself alongside whatever musical identities you care to present to the world, but within reason, and that "reason" is primarily dictated by taste consensus and what is in the shops. We hear that today even in computer and electronically manipulated musics: the imitation of percussive effects, the smears and glitches of sound used in the pockets of the music. Yet theoretically, whatever music you decide to play, percussion can conduct the flow between yourself and the circumstances you live amongst—your environment, mental and physical—colouring the ingredients, and feeding the message. It can make or break the music.

Traditionally, however, in the west and over this last century or so, with the exception of tuned percussion, the instruments of the percussion family seem to have been primarily used as a means of decoration for classical and jazz orchestral work. Big instruments: their function being to colour the main feature, to provide a landscape the other instruments can solo over, or to punctuate ensemble work with suitable sounds. And so on; a secondary role one might say. Gongs, tympani, tubular bells, enormous bass drums, pairs of large orchestral cymbals clashed mightily to signify forces of power and glory. That kind of thing. Even with jazz orchestras one wonders why the huge collections of percussion were really needed. That it looked so spectacular is one thing—a real statement—but how often do we remember Sonny Greer playing the tympani or the tubular bells?

At the other end of the scale, it was not entirely for nothing that the *Leedy Drum Topics* readers would huff and puff to find a new sound from collaborative fiddlings between the shop-bought instruments and the "found" objects of daily life. The silent movies demanded sound to be used in a very particular way. When someone's head is hit with a plank of wood, the foley artist is summoned to recreate the sound. A quick check will tell you that "foley" is used post-production these days, to mainly create the intimate sounds of life's daily details, to sync those sounds with the visual activity. So discovering methods of creating new, isolated sounds in this direction had its merits. But musically? What then? As parlour room entertainment, we could admit of the occasional odd sound—no more curried eggs for you, Mr. Johnson—but to incorporate percussive sounds that step outside the norm and enter into the music itself, we need a music that allows these kinds of things to happen, that allows a vocabulary to be built that can work on a par with the material of the hitherto known "solo" instruments.

The jazz vocabulary, despite its "commitment to improvisation," never really allowed the drummer to fully enter into close dialogue with the lead instruments. The musical hierarchies had been established: the drummer sat at the back. His job, alongside the bass player, was to provide the rhythmic wash that all the others could solo over as the band stuck, more or less rigorously, to the great march of Western Time. We all remember the old adage: "It's a five piece band—four musicians and a drummer." The drummer was allowed to punctuate things, to stir up some action and, post be-bop, to conduct something of the ebb and flow of the music, providing a little dynamic colour, but not really to get inside the music itself and talk closely with the "soloists." It's a music of role playing—very much within a group kind of thing—and of course now primarily a classical music, written down, studied and existing on a plate as material for various repertoires around the globe. We could say that the improvising element has flown out the window, so entirely has the syntax been digested over the decades. Even in the good old days the sheer amount of work placed on soloists, in the orchestras especially, pushed lead soloists towards phrasing that would be quickly remembered and re-hashed. And who could blame them? Arrived at a good solo, why change it?

Improvising has indeed become a very complex term, used more to define a method or process, or even an avoidance.

We can, however, consider that once the syntax has been broken down, musical hierarchies dispatched, and role division removed, we can get on with the process of really making music together. But why should we ever do those things?

Melody could be considered the primary line we traditionally registered in any music. It was always the line that expressed what we wanted to say musically. The other material was essentially the landscape, the environment that supported the melodic line. The musical communion between the two was established by rules, even if it has always been the way in the west to have little concern with an interactivity with environment. The big "I am" stamped its attitude and philosophy on context and all environments irregardless.[7] Indeed, the interaction between the self and the environment in the west has been a story of profound neglect, even as we acknowledge the impact each has on the other. To free improvisation in music-making, this is a crucial issue: context—the who, what, where and when—being a prime agency influencing the nature of output. Even cod-fish develop regional accents, reflecting the nature of the ocean space they inhabit. Birds sing louder in urban settings. The Futurists responded to social and technological changes. Cities have different tempos of life and set the speed of their escalators differently.

We can argue that western music has to a degree lacked this interactive fluidity, demanding, as it does, product above process. Established protocols deep in socio-political cultures short-fuse change, and nowadays the media and taste moguls maintain their crucial part in fixing our business culture, even as so many of us try to break out.

The environment, however, has shifted profoundly, and up to a point, music in the west has responded and pushed at its boundaries. Whilst new ideas were being explored in new composition, pushing at the form, vocabularies and techniques of the classical world, we might be forgiven for considering that jazz in contrast seemed slow to move forward and displace its narrow hierarchies and confining syntax, until social issues and notions of rebellion and freedom started to erupt.[8] Multiple issues disbanded the era of the swing orchestras, and small club be-bop forged new possibilities technically, and to an extent, in the dialogue between rhythm section and soloist. But its role-placement structures remained the same, defining both vocabulary expansions and its restrictions. And rock music's chosen confines as a music of songs, has inevitably seemed to re-enforce a status quo it often wanted to disrupt; and perhaps more so in pop, masquerading short attention spans, and these days short everything. Feel for the poor sweaty drummer stuck at the back, with the unenviable task of slogging out beats to anchor down the music, and perhaps the bank account at the same time. Anyway, machines can do the job; we even witness live music becoming redundant and unnecessary. Even so, too many people make big money out of it still to really shift its structures and fundamental propositions. Or maybe this is just simplistic, convenient thinking? Argue amongst yourselves.

Nevertheless, just as new social developments necessitated the establishment of time cycles and finally the standardising of time itself—so that you knew when you could catch your train to get to work on time—so profound changes in social and environmental conditions have directed developments in music that are hard to ignore.

The development of the internet and the consequent immediacy of information that it offers has finalised a movement towards ease of information-access that often only serious travel could initiate previously. We live in a technologically-mediated environment, and now have knowledge of music and sound created from all parts of the planet. It's an accepted determinant that the interested and curious can hear music from isolated societies far removed from urban life with relative ease; can listen to the recorded sound of insects eating a leaf in the forests and jungles of the world, and can watch Freddie Crump play his teeth with drumsticks on YouTube.[9] All that is needed is the machine called a computer, and the web to plug into.

In the west, our ears have been opened to a vast array of sound information: our environment has changed. As musicians in the midst of all this, how should we respond? What can we do with it all? Do we need to continue being imitators of some other people's musical vocabularies, tweak a little here and there, re-hash our repertoires and collect the dough? Can we re-align or even do away with established musical syntax, and create a music whose grammar allows for a new interactivity?

And when other musicians are expanding vocabularies on their instruments and pushing the boundaries of expression, how can a drummer-percussionist respond?

Can our techniques and our embrace of sound be developed sufficiently, so that we can work with the new vocabularies, and enter into dialogues that switch roles and re-investigate divisions and disband hierarchical structures?

Can the musical syntax for drummers and percussionists be changed so that it is possible—if chosen—to enter into the melodic line and play inside the detail of the music?

And so this book isn't simply a display of alternative sounds as an impetus for a bit of urban foraging, but hopefully a stimulus for new approaches to physical technique and ear technique in the 21st century. Perhaps also rethinking what a group of musicians in the west is allowed to be, opening up instrumentation, breaking down deadlocks in who is allowed to do what.

But it is also—as you may gather—very much aimed at enjoyment. Making music can be very hard work, but it should nevertheless be a pleasure.

My guess is I found the bowl in this bowl-spring combination at my local street market, which still happens to be the Portobello Road market in west London. It's the kind of shopping I've always preferred, allowing chance and cheapness to accommodate each other. I originally used the bowl as a kind of western version of a singing-bowl, which in turn was used primarily for meditation in India and latterly in the west. This kitchen version, often available in a group of different sized bowls, was a cheap way of getting varied pitches according to size, and a rounded but muted tonal quality less recognisable than the clear registers of the singing bowl. These kitchen instruments cannot be made to sound by friction, as with the singing bowls, partly because they are made of a chromed alloy, but also because their lip flange curves outward. However, you fortunately needn't be overly concerned about playing them with mallets and sticks because they don't crack easily as the singing bowls can. Those are made with an easily-fractured alloy and, especially if you have a good one, must be treated with the utmost care.

These more mundane bowls are nothing new amongst certain percussionists who are also familiar with using such things as car hub-caps as suspended gongs. You can drill a hole in the centre of these bowls and suspend them or put them on the floor or other surface, upside down or as normal. But I had this large spring, I think from the suspension system of a light motorbike. How I came across it I don't really remember, but I'm guessing I found it in the street, in those days when useful things could still be found, long before the etiquettes of street hygiene—both visual and health-specific—removed all such goodies from western sensibilities. I also remember I wasn't sure how best to use it.

One of the major obstacles for drummers and percussionists has been to find the most practical and acoustically best way to mount the various sound-sources they use, a problem which is then magnified when one has to consider transport. And multiplied even more so if one has to fly. This issue of carrying and transporting one's instruments can have its advantages, however. It became a centrally defining criterion for me in deciding what and how much to use, and so has been enormously influential in both the decisions I made and how I approached the problems inherent in playing the instruments themselves. "More from less" almost became a rallying cry.

It was for this reason that I started using a floor kit—putting all percussion instruments on the floor, and playing from a kneeling position. Very interesting initially, because, as discussed elsewhere, the geography of the instruments can be changed mid performance. You can literally shift the groupings of instruments as and if you want, which gives you advantages with texture and pitch clusters.

Well, for many reasons, there's a limit to how long you might want to be doing that. It's not the manipulation of sounds that is the problem, but the being on your knees. Playing concerts before large audiences on your knees in front of piles of junk can erode the vanities of self-esteem as well as actually hurt. The physical toll is real. Fortunately, the issues of how much I could cram into a bass drum case to take onto an aeroplane took over, and I began to ditch the idea of being a gremlin ferreting away amongst a field of percussion. It was clearly an approach which for me stopped working when I realised I couldn't carry the necessary quantity of instruments needed. The actual approach itself became redundant.

However, with this particular instrument I decided to put the spring on the bowl, and let the bowl act as a resonator, a simple solution for disparate entities that sonically really work together.

As with many of the others, I've had this instrument since the mid 1970s, and when put on the surface of my dear old Meazzi pedal tom, it can attain that kind of industrially cosmic thing about its sound, that interplanetary kitchen thing we have all relished since the late 1960s... haven't we? No, of course not. Yet together with its visual qualities and design mechanics, we could now perhaps talk about it as an "urban fountain of aural delight" instrument... we could, but are far too embarrassed... Anyway, it is still virtually impossible for me to take to any concert outside London. Such a daft shape.

I called this "the zed spring," and found it in a road side skip. It's a piece of galvanised, semi spring-tensioned steel, which I bent in the middle to give it the form of a set of prongs. It can then be placed on a surface to play, with one side free to be manipulated for sound and pitch possibilities, or simply held in the hand, struck or bowed or have its edges rubbed with a long, thin metal rod to catch a fine, accurate sustain, very useful for percussionists.

In many ways this instrument is similar to the musical saw, having a tensioned pliancy that gives it some of the note-bending facility the musical saw has. The zed spring is far more limited though, but—a notable positive—it is far easier to pack and carry!

A kind of small percussive colander, this is useful for putting things in and shaking them about. And because it has a hard metallic shell that resonates well, you can even put one solitary thing in it, and of course this thing can be changed at whim, making it very simple but quite versatile. Coins, keys, stones, seeds, nails, bones, paper…etc. You can also turn it over and play its flat surface to get a hard, metallic sound.

Having containers that can also behave as instruments—or vice versa—is actually very useful, and I also have a wood block that is fashioned as a box that I use often. One can put smaller percussive items inside to shake or spill out whilst one is using the main body of the container as an instrument to play in itself. This facilitates speed and the shaping of ideas within line playing, and helps the movement of texture within clear, struck sounds to be more interesting.

It's the sort of object you could almost keep in your pocket, but—of course—would never dream of doing so. Why would you?

JUNK

This photo shows the reverse side of a green plastic dinner table mat of the kind found in one pound coin shops. It's cut out of a larger ribbed mat so that it can fit on the playing surface of a drum and not take up all the space.

The ribbing on these is the important thing, as well as the fact that it's made from some kind of plastic, the hardness of which helps define its sound. The ribbing is preferably quite fine and dense, which allows the mat to be swished over with a stick of some kind, producing a sound not unlike that from a DJ or turntable specialist when they're scratching a disc. Used like this, it becomes an instrument that maybe helps blur the boundaries not just between instruments of fundamentally different kinds, but also acoustic from electric or even electronic instruments.

It's interesting to acknowledge that percussion really has the capability of getting inside certain electronic and also vocal sounds, opening up textures and dialogues and musical possibilities. Blurring distinctions between instruments may not necessarily be a laudable aim, but being able to bridge those distinctions in a fluid way or do the opposite and reinforce them, can really help music work its mysterious path. Some like to consider percussion as a decorator's tool, but of course to those blessed with serious ears and a perceptive mind, it is far more than that. I remember standing on the pavement one afternoon in west London with John Stevens when his taxi arrived. While giving instructions to the cabbie, he made sure all was understood by declaring forcefully that we were percussionists, and so—the implication was—the cabbie had better watch out and behave accordingly. And it's the same with music.

So, why take a photo of the reverse side of this mat thing? Well, the other side was just much less interesting to look at. And, being made of plastic, over the years it had cracked a couple of times, so

JUNK

I've used my favourite means of solving life's practical problems and gaffa-taped over the cracks. Wherever you go in life, carry gaffa tape.

I made the cymbals in the first photo (p. 31) from sheet brass at an adult education centre near where I lived in London in the 1970s. I was so desperate for large, dome-belled cymbals that I enrolled at the institute's metal workshop where I set about making my own.

It was fantastic to do this, heating and hammering the brass on heavy leather pouches filled with sand. They didn't have cymbal-smith anvils, naturally enough, so I had to get on with this method to shape and give tension to the alloy.

The cymbals in the second photo (p. 32) have been re-hammered from commercial cymbals made from either brass or a thin nickel-silver alloy. I re-hammered these later to improve their sonic properties, a successful attempt to make them more interesting to play.

Brass cymbals (an alloy of copper and zinc) are interesting because they give a different response to the stick. It's less giving to the touch; more direct, harder and less complex in tone.

Perhaps because cymbals are considered non-pitched instruments—too complex, by far—in a sense our "ears" have been conditioned in their responses to assert brass as possibly less "interesting" or less "musical" even—if we can ever say such a thing. But, having said such a thing, to my ears the difference allows interest, the alloy's limitations setting up a constant tension between what is and what is not present in the cymbal's sound, and this gives it something special to offer in the spectrum of a percussionist's vocabulary.

Needless to say, anything which questions the normalisation of sound—and here, I mean the way we have been taught to consider and accept sound by the music industry in total—may well be a useful tool for generating other ideas and vocabularies. However, not fitting into a commodifiable musical package does have its drawbacks: one has to figure things out for oneself. But do not fret: Hugo Pinksterboer's opening sentence in his book on cymbals makes the all-justifying claim that," the characteristic tendency of drummers to try out any given object that might possibly produce a musical sound dates from a long time ago."[10] Clearly, our book here is concerned both with the nature of those objects and indeed in exploring just what a "musical sound" may be, or rather, in discovering whether it is ever possible to have a sound that is not potentially "musical"...

What is termed the B20 cymbal alloy (80% copper and 20% tin), considered as the fundamental alloy ratio used by the great Turkish cymbal-makers long ago and used as a basis by the majority of makers today, does however furnish the most incredibly complex instruments. A good cymbal is in its acoustic, sonic structure an exceptionally complex thing, and in its seemingly supreme simplicity of form, extremely beautiful. How lucky we drummers and percussionists are to be playing such things.

However, this isn't the place to discuss further about all this. We would be here for a very long time indeed...

JUNK

I like these very much. They are three round slices of solid aluminium I got from the floor of a metal stockist's warehouse somewhere off Ludgate Hill, if memory serves me well. Certainly somewhere in London EC1. This place was my prime source of metal off-cuts in the late 1970s, the other being a far smaller stockist's in Chiswick, surprisingly enough.

And then there is also a very beautiful, pale-blue aluminium saucepan lid in the first photo (p. 35) that I drilled a hole through so that I could mount it mainly on the top of a flat ride cymbal to add to the cymbal's pitch range and give it some extra jangle if so desired. This is an incredibly sonorous instrument, very different in character from the small heavy Chinese cymbals that are so popular, but is perhaps less suited to manipulations to bend its sound. Very special nevertheless.

Indeed, these discs have all the qualities of aluminium I like: a specific sonority not to be confused with brass, far drier with less projection; relatively lightweight, but solid.

The flat discs measure 14cms, 15cms, and 16cms x1. I found myself using these almost exclusively on the surface of a snare drum or tom-tom, providing a clean, pointillist sound in the mix of phrasing and in the midst of lines played on the drums and other metal percussive surfaces. The great thing with these discs also is that they lie flat on the surface of a drumhead, don't bounce when struck and so create a sound with precise definition, and—importantly—also act as dampers to change the resonance of the drum itself, adding a dryness to much of the various textures and pitches that would be alerted in the course of playing. This allowed an extremely useful level of clarity to fast phrasing and runs on the instruments.

Consequently, I used these discs a lot, and one in particular shows evidence of being struck not only with sticks but also with heavier metallic beaters. It almost looks hammered...

JUNK

Aaah…This is really an old friend (p. 39). Every gig I have done in my life for two or three decades, big and small, this cymbal has been with me.

It's pretty much a conventional cymbal, except of course, it isn't.

It's been hand made from brass, and not by a particularly skilled maker but, more likely, by someone trying their luck at making a cymbal. Strangely enough, I also tried this long ago—before forming the large-domed cymbals I mentioned earlier—also with brass, and my home-made efforts were as rough and misshapen as this cymbal is. Like so many items in my percussion collection, I found this in my local street market long ago, paid very little for it, and have loved it ever since. Its sound is less cleanly ringing than the standardised small and heavy Wuhan cymbals appreciated by just about every improvising and even classical percussionist on the planet. Quite rightly so. I love them, too, and they're great. But their cutting kind of clarity can seem overstated and predictable, whereas my little bit of brass is not. It's a gem, surprisingly discreet and mellow, but it can also raunch with the best of them and lead the way.

I made and put a particular handle on this cymbal—and others—so that I can pick it up easily, control its position on a drum head accurately with one hand, and strike it with a stick in the other. Using it on a snare drum surface can give a great deal of intricacy and texture to one's playing, but best of all is its use on my old Meazzi pedal tom, where the pitch can be altered and the sound of the cymbal shaped very subtly. That combination is extremely special to me, giving so many exciting and precise musical options.

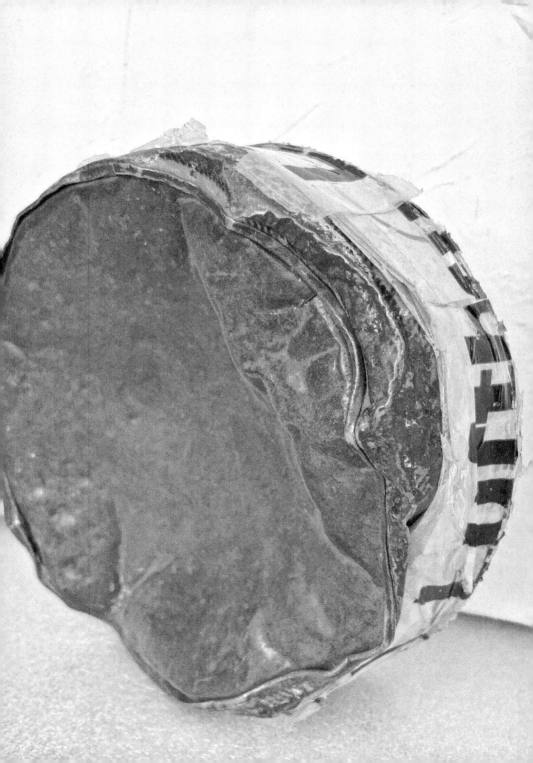

JUNK

This (p. 41) is a round tartan tin with a handful of one centimetre ball bearings inside. Like the brass sheet we will come across later, it was once part of the floor kit that I used primarily with the singer Phil Minton, and it has suffered from some stringent use.

It is an instrument I enjoyed a lot because it could be played as a drum, sounding like a small but slightly crazed snare drum, contained and dry and very useful therefore in the context of fast line-playing, where excessive resonance could be a problem. But then, picked up and shaken or shifted side to side on the floor, it would sound like an attack of heavy hail on a tin roof, a great ingredient when a barrage texture was needed.

I remember one occasion when a customs officer in a U.S airport was concerned about the tin and its contents, and I had to take it apart for inspection. He couldn't find the weapon, talking insistently about a musket for the ammunition inside my suitcase, and seemed unwilling to grasp my concept of "percussion." I remember wondering if he was one of those re-enactors of the Civil War, when the Springfield and Enfield percussion muskets were just about all that "percussion" was ever allowed to signify (at a time when American rudimental snare drumming was so much part of the lexicon of communication and fear). Well, anyway... not wishing to reference any actual wars, I put some Lufthansa sticky tape round the tin to reassure any future customs officer inquiries, and to stop the lid from coming off of course... Strangely, it looks much friendlier, and I have never had similar problems with the tin since... (*Deutschland über alles*, after all.)

JUNK

This (p. 43) is a squashed-up sheet of something like matte black lead. I'm not sure of the alloy, except that it is possible to scrunch it and then open it back up, albeit with the creases still found within it. It's a great product and was given to me by the dancer and choreographer Josef Nadj, who was using sheets of it in the production I worked in briefly.

It's not really a sound producer in itself. It's more a sound activator—a device for producing sound out of other things through rubbing and scraping. That kind of manual application some percussionists get very involved with. It's ok, but somehow maybe not so healthy…

This kind of instrument, found in these photos (pp. 45- 46), could fundamentally be a piece of scrap metal of any kind—maybe brass, aluminium or a basic steel. I have bent these two pieces into shapes that allow a wider variety of sound to be produced and which make it possible to place on other surfaces to play.

Often, metal pieces like these would be placed on a drum surface, using this as a resonator to help the sound project and have a little more life. Drums used as table-surface resonators are a common-enough feature with both drummers and percussionists these days, and this practice makes it possible for the player to manipulate the sounds manually whilst working the instrument with a stick or whatever beater is chosen. Metal used this way comes up with surprising results, less sophisticated and less predictable than many professional metallophone equivalents, and can perhaps coax more interest out of both the player and the listener therefore.

As with many metal bar or metal plate instruments, you can also use a piece of foam rubber placed under it to help stabilise and also resonate the instrument's sound. I used this technique often when setting up a floor kit because it greatly enhances sound projection, which can be both one of the main hindrances to playing floor percussion as well as one of its attributes. For fast kaleidoscopic detail, a lack of resonance in metal percussion can often be an advantage, especially when working in tandem inside the detail of low-volume acoustic instruments. Nevertheless, the use of foam rubber is also extremely beneficial if one is arranging percussion to be played on a table-top. Hard surfaces can kill the resonance of, for example, most flat metal instruments.

Not a pocket Anthony Caro rip-off sculpture, but a piece of elegant nonsense I seem almost to never use. It works... It definitely has a sound, but in the context of live music-making, it feels too fiddly to get to unless space and time prevail correctly, and it's maybe too lumpy to carry around for the qualities it offers.

However, it is a good idea, using springs with a resonating structure that can even be mounted on a cymbal stand. One could almost imagine that one of these drum/percussion companies would jump at it and market it in Day-Glo purple with a series of L.A session hairdos twinkling it on YouTube. This one is metal and a bit rusty, and I really like it sitting in unfathomable silence on its shelf... waiting.

What we see here is a saucepan lid… a device I like very much. I use this very specifically, not to strike with a stick or metal needle, but either to dig into and work the inside of with a table fork—keeping the domestic theme alive, you see—or to use frictionally around the rim of a rotating cymbal. Both actions result in great sounds and could be achieved using a small cymbal, but the resulting sounds would be no way nearly as effective. Using the bottom edge that enables the lid to fit inside the saucepan's rim gives it a sharp resonance against the rotating cymbal.

The idea of spinning a cymbal on its stand and holding something like this against its rim is another method I used to create extended sounds out of certain percussion, in the way that bowing a cymbal might be used to achieve. In this instance, though, the sound is of a thin, sharply resonant metal against the more sophisticated resonance of a cymbal. The effect cuts the nerves, like a piece of industrial machinery in loud searing operation, but can also give a softer hiss as a backdrop for other instruments to play over.

I notice now, after years of effort to get cymbals to spin on their stands, that a company has come up with a small device that uses ball-bearings—as in roller skates—to enable cymbals to be spun very freely. Nice idea.

JUNK

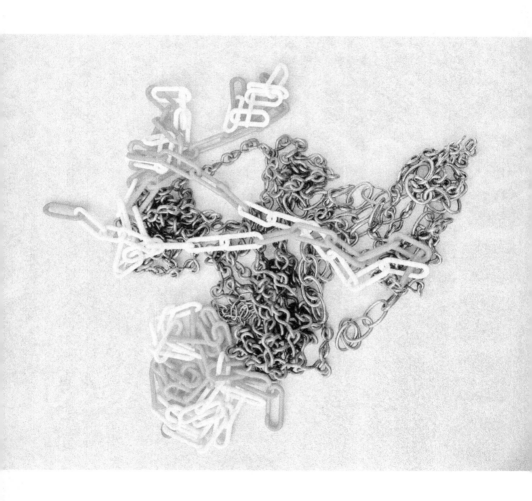

We are not really supposed to find chains amusing. Historically, they have a lot to answer for, being instrumental to the deprivations of a great many people throughout the world.

But when I have been using them for percussion, I must say that I often find them hilarious. There's nothing that brings a bigger smile to my face than dumping a handful of chain on a snare drum to wreak some kind of musical havoc on whatever's going on—or not going on—in the musical momentum. Sometimes, I even caught band members aghast at the sheer audacity of playing chains in our music, the non-musical musicality upsetting their delicacies or the harmonious boredom of music that—let's be honest—can sometimes get close to withering our souls. Chains are the go-to instrument to stir up some action.

Well, that's part of the story anyway. Texturally, they are, in fact, great. Dangled and rubbed over a drumhead or any metal at all, they offer a kind of fundamental roll, a journey to the subterranean depths that a simple rattle can't reach. They really can offer an avalanche of indiscretion that has a real musical place. And they can be jingled carefully in the hand to create a kind of rain-on-the-roof atmosphere, or, maybe with dancers, used as an aberrant snake on the floor, creating swirls and patterns of movement trailing across a space.

I have been told that the percussionist and drummer Tony Oxley had been known to use chains, but I never witnessed this myself. Personally, I doubt very much he would have ever used them when playing with Cecil Taylor, Cecil being very often a fast, fluid moving––even swinging—pianist, though some might disagree with that. "Some," in this instance, might include the great singer Betty Carter, who lived in Cecil's neighbourhood in Brooklyn. They crossed paths one day in the street, and exchanged greetings:

"Hello CT," quoth Miss Carter. "How're you keeping?"

"Hello Betty," says Cecil. "Well, you know... still swinging."

"Cecil," replied the sardonic Miss B, "you wouldn't swing if they hung you."

In any case, I would prefer to think: no chains for CT, and when I had the great fortune to play with Cecil he was certainly travelling at a speed that would have rendered chain-usage a severe impediment! Safety first: they might have tied me in knots. But chains clearly, within the horrors of race history, were just not something to deploy with black American jazz artists. I would never have dreamt of massaging my drumset with a handful of chains when Charles Gayle especially was in full cry. Charles could really make you feel the depth of his belonging, the pain of walking his long road. White people can hang their heads and shudder abysmally in response.

Anyway, and notwithstanding, you need a reasonably medium gauge chain, not a lightweight trinket, and you need one made with good steel. They really can sound better, one from another, and it's worth hunting to find a good one at a suitable length—two or three metres or more. Sometimes, chains for musical use have been adapted to handles so that each hand can control lengths of chain, their ends suspended and dragged over various types of surfaces——metal plates, cymbals, collections of suitable objects, and even drums.

Chains can be heard in compositions like Varese's Integrales and Milhaud's Les Choephores, but were perhaps first used in the west as percussion by Schoenberg in the Gurrelieder (1911). The 1925 Varese composition is, of course, extraordinary. Amongst other instrumentalists, it demands four percussionists, of which one is responsible for sleigh bells, tambourine, a gong and tam-tam, and chains.

In 1925, whilst Varese was cutting loose his four percussionists and chains, Duke Ellington's Orchestra was stepping in time either as the "Jungle Band" or as the Cotton Club Orchestra. In 1929, it would record "High Life," with Sonny Greer playing deft and beautiful tubular bells. How amazing that this early orchestral jazz could be so focused and cleanly melodic, when Varese was ripping up the soundwaves with the turbulence of urban life. And, of course, many will now love both—I certainly do—but had I been alive then, who knows? It's quite possible that the Atlantic Ocean, plus the informational lapses of the time, would have prevented almost all of us from hearing either, perhaps especially us in the U.K.

As cultural challenges go, one can be sure Varese's piece would have been the most difficult to commodify. One didn't go out dancing to Varese, and conversely, neither could one depend on a grounding of imaginative interest from those considered to be in the know or loosely on your side. Narrow and blinkered opinions will always have their day. Many years after Varese's compositions were available, new explorations were still under attack. "Did you ever conduct any Stockhausen, Sir Thomas?" came the question.

"No, but I believe I've trod in some," came Beecham's reply.[11]

With history as a complex piece of circuitry, and warfare big and small as an effervescent conductor of cultural traits, the U.K., despite its vegetarians, so-called eccentrics, opium dens, and gin palaces, and despite the momentum of its sense of humour, seems ever reluctant to embrace a culture that allows one to sniff much freedom of expression. Not unless, of course, it brings in the money first...

But the corollary to this may be that we have produced some of the most amazingly investigative and exhilarating musics on the planet in other ways.

JUNK

I like this tin box (p. 59) of old toy rattles and bones. They are put together in there because they fit, and because they are almost never taken out to use anymore.

The rattles came from the alto saxophone player, Gary Hassay, after a gig in Allentown, U.S.A. with Phil Minton. I remember someone German in the audience referring to us as "lumpen proletariat" and thinking how strange to dredge up the steel town's past by referring to improvising musicians in this way, especially as I remember floating polystyrene packing chips that I had found in a great cloud in the air with a hand-held battery fan during the concert with Phil—a somewhat surreal visual and auditory dance that perhaps challenged or caused offence to that particular "audience."

Anyway, the rattles are a bit too fragile to use much, and the bones demanded more from me than my mortal flesh could happily muster, so, like the spoons, were never truly done justice to by myself. Their history and they themselves remain parked in their little tin coffin, behaving dutifully to remind the children's toy rattles what the future holds. Apropos of which, I remember Gary came out of the U.S.A. army post-Vietnam and, I believe, dug a deep hole in the ground somewhere to bury weapons in. Solid.

JUNK

This (p. 61) is special and, coming from the long legacy of Gamelan instruments, cannot be considered to be of the junk persuasion.

A long time ago, I bought an entire set of *gendèr* instruments from someone in London who no longer had use for them. I had admired not just the sound but also the blade-like quality of this instrument ever since I first heard gamelan music and knew of these bars. There is a beautiful weighty finesse about them, and one can sense in the honing of each blade the passage of time taken to perfect their sound. They are really fantastic.

But what to do with them? I don't know how many I have, but there are two heavy bundles wrapped in the same paper I received them in when I went to collect them, and even the smallest/shortest is a heavy item.

At first, I would take a few with me to certain concerts, primarily in London, considering their weight when travelling. I would play them one or two at a time, quickly laying them on drum heads for a short passage where their distinctive sound would be welcome but not overt, maybe for pitch as much as anything, offering a clear note value in the midst of sometimes complex textures or interwoven lines.

Then I started to place them on foam rubber rectangles that could be easily carried and quickly placed on surfaces. And finally, as all this proved too arduous and complicated to set up in the middle of a concert (space, speed, ever-changing percussive geographies, the need to abandon frames and permanent fixtures to hang or support instruments from, taking precedence over everything), I started to use three or four bars only and backed each with slices of foam rubber tacked with double-sided tape so that the bars could resonate. This worked especially when placed on a drum surface, and I still often carry just one or two of the largest bars with the deeper pitches to play. They can really underpin certain low-volume music with their rich sonority.

Eventually, I decided to also use a small construction like you see in the photo for certain situations, primarily where no air travel was required. This provides me with enough bars to set up a fuller rhythmic-melodic texture, which I can again render less overt (as in a less culturally-appropriating approach) by adapting and preparing if I choose. Laying other metal across certain bars to manipulate their sound or scraping lightly with other thin metals—hence the set squares—is a way to offset this musical theft.

Personally, I believe we have to be careful with how we use instruments from other cultures. Cultural colonising is a tricky and complex issue, and the theft of other people's musical and visual material—primarily by the west—is something to avoid at all costs. I remember in Australia seeing LP's of didgeridoo music carrying clear instruction as to the circumstances in which the LP's music should and should not be played. To enjoy, study, and be influenced by the music of other nations is doubtless a great thing however, and how much greater this would be if it brought the peoples of the world into a closer understanding and respect for each other.

Having said all this, it's clear to me that I got great inspiration from some of the village gong music from the Philippines, its amazing rattling dissonances behind the solo *kolintang* player insistent and almost nutty. A very interesting form of gamelan music.

This is simple but interesting because it has evolved from a variety of sources, none of which in a way actually fit.

Originally it was an aluminium tube—one of many that I cut to use as an instant xylophone. And then there is a spring that I believe was once part of broken, muscle-training western sports/torture equipment I found dumped in the street, which I claimed for the spring itself. And finally, as you can readily see, there is a quite large, right-angled set-square.

The spring needed fixing to something at both ends before it would resonate. Springs are very interesting items, sound-wise, but this one is quite loose and lanky, so has its own particular needs when it comes to housing it. Luckily, the length of tubing is sufficient to provide it with almost enough tension when the spring is fixed to it at both ends for it to be twanged or played frictionally. And the pipe, being hollow, allows a certain amount of resonance. But none of these things proved enough. What I needed to do was set a bridge under the spring, as in a double bass or any conventional string instrument, and elevate it so that it could really be twanged. Having done this, what then could I twang it with? Well, the set square lent itself to the cause, and if a drumstick isn't handy then the set square offers a certain kind of glassiness to the sound of the spring, especially when the end of the tube is held against a resonant surface to help enrich and project the sound. Additionally, and importantly, the set square will not get trapped in between the coils of the spring as a long needle might do, but neither should a drumstick. However, the sound is better... The bridge is a short length of thin but rigid plastic tubing.

Following instructions from the Washington Military Training Program mentioned in the introduction, I can only conclude that this kind of instrument would be ideal for the United States Army, or indeed any army of the world. The set square—though not essential—would signify enough cerebral status, stiffening the resolve to manage the challenge. The entire instrument could be used whilst marching, adding a new development to the "shoulder arms" instruction bellowed into already defeated ears. Perhaps a suitable tune could be whistled by the entire regiment during this ritual, something like Ornette Coleman's "The Legend of Bebop," perhaps; something to change the sensibility and thinking of the entire army... and persuade them all to listen to the everlasting beauty of Ed Blackwell's drumming.

JUNK

These (p. 67) are interesting partly because they are at once an instrument and can as well be used to strike certain instruments like a stick would be used. They function in both ways.

I searched for this material for a long time, looking for a plastic with a certain reverberating buoyancy, and eventually came across a shop in New York by total accident that had these long plastic tubes stacked in a bin of some sort outside on the pavement. They are made of a thin plastic that can crack relatively easily if mistreated but, when they are cut to length, can produce very beautiful and mellow tones with a bouncing roundness and mellifluousness that a marimba would struggle to achieve.

Plastic is another material that has true, albeit complex, potential for both the future percussionist and composer. As a material for musical instruments, it has been explored before. We find it in the famous Grafton saxophone, first produced in London in 1950, long enough ago for Charlie Parker and then Ornette Coleman to play, and then there have been plastic sousaphones, and now plastic cornets and euphoniums, and I even saw a white plastic double bass long ago in the Palais Des Beaux Arts in Brussels. But for found instruments and percussion in general, it feels it has not really been developed enough. There are plastic "wood" blocks and a couple of shake-type manufactured things, but for our focus on found instruments, it seems that maybe there are not the objects out in the world that have that specific potential. It's hard to get a workable sound out of a plastic model Superman— except, perhaps, by crushing it underfoot— but, stepping into the debate around plastics and single-use plastic containers, place-mats, bottles, forks, and maybe even plates can all have their musical uses. I have to say, I use plastic cymbals created for either practice or T.V. miming, in certain musical situations. They offer a very flat, dead resonance that I have found extremely useful. Great for be-bop!

These particular tubes, used carefully, can be played on or used as self-sounding beaters that simply need to be played on any surface—a table, the ground, the hoops of a drum, a cymbal—to either add to that surface's sound or simply to resonate themselves.

They are very light to transport, need protection in packing, but they are wine-gum red!

JUNK

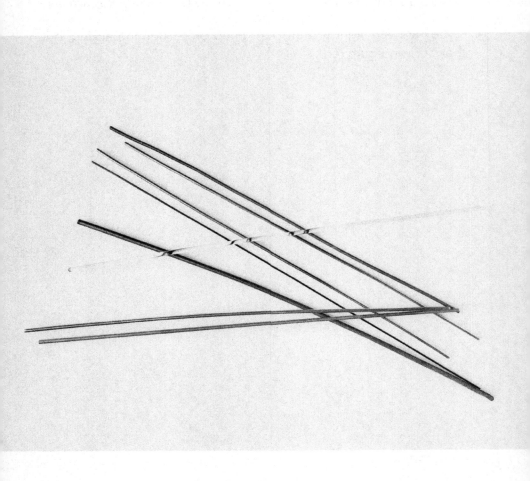

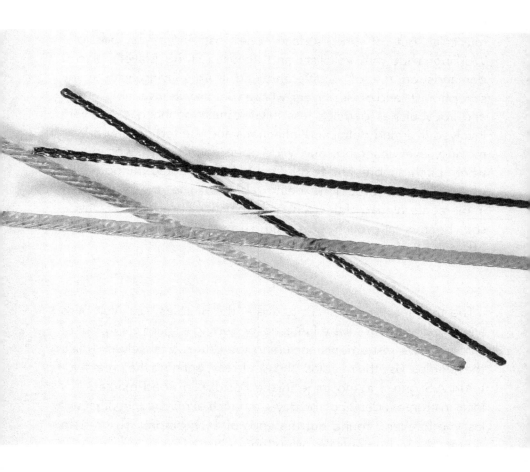

JUNK

These are some of the implements I use to strike, rub, scratch, glide across, or by some manner of means draw a sound out of other percussion instruments. Hitting them, mainly. They have been incredibly important to me because they became part of my research, experimenting with finding ways of getting as much musically out of one surface—one instrument—as possible. Working a lot with vocalists and acoustic string players placed demands on me of a different kind from playing with many saxophonists and brass players, whose volume was invariably louder and vocabularies perhaps less micro-tonally nuanced. I got very involved in sound detail and inflections and wanted to offer a fast-moving, ever-changing, and wide-open sound-scape vocabulary where pitch, timbre, and texture could be respected during flights of speed and precision. Being able to use these different implements instead of the standard drumsticks, brushes and maybe soft beaters approach gave me choices I would never have otherwise had.

The thin, long metal sticks I have—"the needles," as Alan Silva always called them—were fantastic for getting a sharp clarity out of all percussive instruments, including the drums themselves. "I like the needles. Use the needles," he would say, grinning the great two-teeth A.S grin. I found mine in the Portobello Road market—my local instrument dealer of the day— a bunch of maybe thirty that will last me forever. I round out the ends of each before use, to help protect the instruments I'm using them with.

In all the years of performing with these, however, I don't think I've ever split a drumhead or cracked anything with them. You have to be careful, but not so cautious that it gets in the way of the music. They give a great pointillist quality to playing if one needs to go down that path, giving a sharp, accurate definition to individual strikes on any percussion instrument or drum, but also allowing particular kinds of attack to especially metal—rubbing, glancing glissandi or striking notes.

JUNK

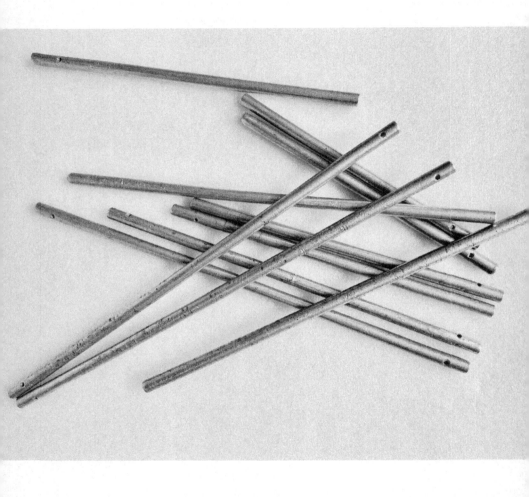

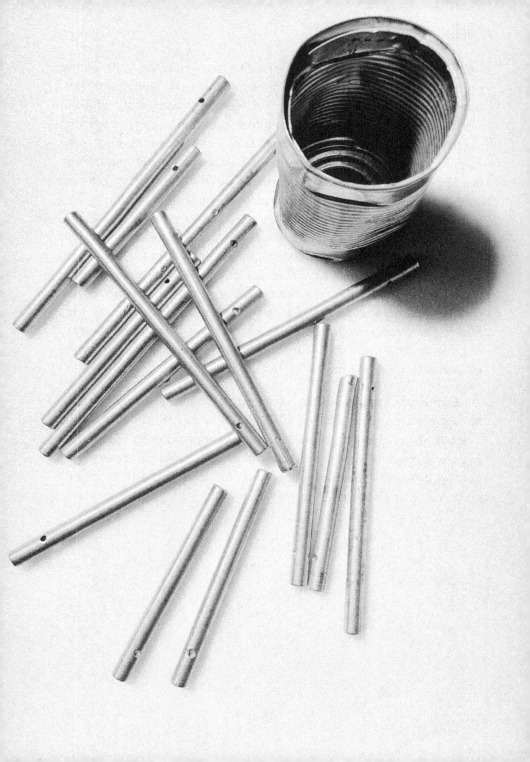

JUNK

Whilst these (p. 74 and 75) look like they may be part of the percussionist's stick equipment, these are actually aluminium rods, cut to different lengths that act as metallophones with different pitches. I made them because I wanted something easy to carry that could be used like a xylophone, but without the cumbersome carrying and setting-up problems inevitable with that instrument. Equally important was the fact that they were cut to random pitches, so that microtonal shifts could be played rather than labouring with a standardised western scale. The rods, however, only half-solved the problem, firstly because they were of low volume, and secondly because to get them to resonate they needed to be placed on something like foam rubber. This was not necessarily a problem, as foam rubber is easy to carry. But to get set up when playing a basic drumset during a concert and at speed was not always so easy. They had to be spread separate from each other—to maximize clarity of sound—on the right sort of resonant surface, and sang best when played with a thinner metal "stick."

Eventually, I learnt to take advantage of the tendency of the rods to wobble around and fall by making the falling an effective sound in itself. A bunch of these rods carefully dropped onto a surface— maybe a piece of metal or a cymbal even—could produce a very cutting but somehow melodic sound. Juggled in the hand or in a container was also very effective.

JUNK

This (p. 77) is really an *anti*-cheesegrater. Maybe not so easy to see, but all its sides have been hammered flat to avoid unsightly accidents.

It's one thing to shock an audience musically, but quite another to grate your fingers in front of them and squirt blood over the front row. So, not entirely for convenience sake, this piece of essentially culinary equipment has been totally re-hammered. By "re-hammered," I mean not by drumsticks during the course of actually playing and hitting the thing, but re-hammered as in making all the sharp bits totally flat and harmless by hitting it with a hammer, with care and... finesse. I have an old cobbler's anvil at home, so I put the grater over one of the sections and gave it a good walloping with a heavy hammer. Such joy!

So it is a non-cheesegrater that still retains the iconoclastic look of the classic device. Very crafty.

The instrument—for it deserves to be called so—is perhaps best played with my long fine needles, giving it a dulled yet pointillist sound quality which is why I keep it and occasionally bring it out for use to loud applause. Some may think the sound... grates somewhat... Oh dear... But I certainly think it's great... etc.

Best thing is, it has a handle that works.

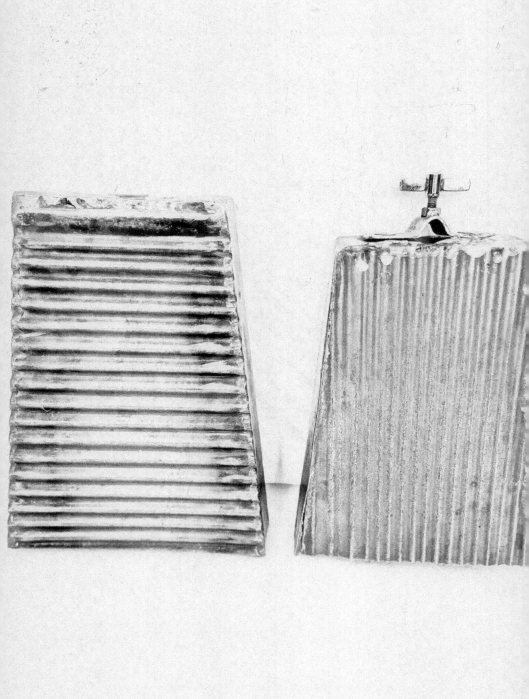

JUNK

The flat, ribbed cowbells and the ribbed brass plates (pp. 79-81) came from a blacksmith based on the edge of a small village 50-60k outside Stockholm. I was taken to visit him by the pianist, Arne Forsen, who knew I had eyes and ears for such stuff. It would have been in 1997. Going to the blacksmith's workshop was fantastic, like entering a mediaeval warehouse of torture: huge iron devices with cogs to turn with cumbersome steering wheels and fearful creakings, a smell of oil and heated metals. The blacksmith showed me how to rib pieces of metal, and I was able to transform one or two simple rectangles of brass or steel while he himself made me the brass and steel cowbells, stamping his initials YN and the year '97 into the metals. A really generous soul, able to goad his bulky old machinery into the fine arts of percussion-making…

Ribbed metal allows the percussionist to sustain a sound otherwise primarily only allowed by playing a rudimental roll with sticks or fingers, or by bowing something like a cymbal or other suitable—and usually—metal instruments. I always carry the small brass-ribbed plate to work, and it's been in and out of my case all over the world. At some point, I fixed a strip of foam rubber along the back to give the plate more resonance, but later have preferred to play it flat on the surface of a drum, or at angles to vary the sound. It is also effective when balanced on the palm of the hand, allowing a clear vibrance to its sound and giving the audience a chance to see clearly the instrument that makes the sound. That occasional focus is useful.

That's a broken brass sheet (p. 83) that was once a perfect rectangle. Heavily hammered to produce that heavily-hammered sound that only a broken brass sheet can give...(no coughing at the back there)... I put a hole in the middle with the idea to suspend it like a cymbal, but never really bothered to try that more than once.

Let's not forget, though, that sheets of metal were used to produce something close to the sound of thunder both in theatre productions and, no doubt, in certain orchestral compositions. Surely the witches in "Macbeth" were dancing round their pots to the tantalising sounds produced by an enormous sheet of thin metal being hammered by a backstage maestro.

However, one cannot easily persuade either venue budgets or the air companies themselves that get you to the concert or gig to transport such an item for you... And this indeed is an interesting area for the percussionist to probe, and one that can absorb a great deal of consideration throughout his or her life, depending on musical choices, status, and the economics thereof: how to balance practicalities with musical needs, and how to do so as one gets older?

And so the small brass sheet has become a reduction both in size and in sound. No longer a thunder sheet, it has become a source for a kind of trashy rattle, like a loose snare drum with a strange form of metallic diarrhea, or, when placed on a drum and hit quite hard with a single stroke, can produce a dirty, brassy snare drum backbeat to puncture everyone's sense of decency. No more curried eggs for that percussionist!

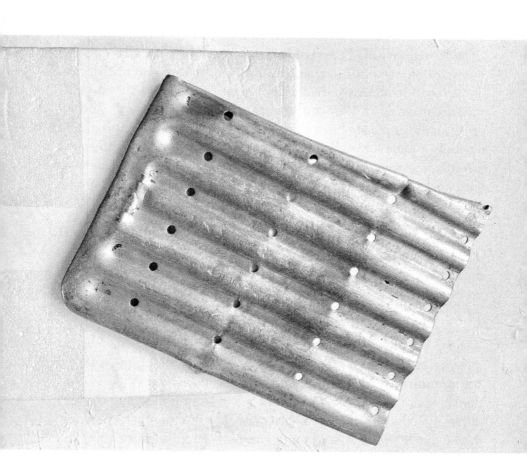

JUNK

This (p. 85) is a piece of aluminium I would guess taken from a rack from some kind of cooker. It came from Martin Davidson's collection that he brought with him from Australia on his move back to the U.K.[12] I think Martin would have suspended this from one of his frames, but I used it either on a drum surface or on a piece of foam rubber. In either case, very much horizontally.

I liked this instrument particularly because it introduced me to the merits of aluminium compared with the usual attractions of brass and bronze in the percussionist's arsenal. Aluminium still remains the great unsung alloy for the percussionist, although certain companies like Paiste have started using it in the production of bell cymbals. Aluminium is first of all light, so is easier to transport. But for me, its primary benefit lies in the tonal quality it offers: a flattened, drier quality that projects less vividly, but consequently gives a slightly rounded tonality.

This particular piece of aluminium, however, has another quality I discovered in playing, one that not only influenced and opened up the way I began to use drumsticks and all manner of strikers and beaters, but also caused me to discover and investigate other instruments perhaps modified to make more of this quality possible.

This piece of metal is ribbed, and it was this that opened up so many possibilities for my percussive vocabulary, being my first real confrontation with an object with that particular shaping. I realised that if I learnt to play the instrument in a left-to-right gliding motion, rather than the vertical strike of all drumstick rudimental techniques, then I could hold a lengthened tone akin to a drum roll. The technique of horizontal motion has been a great contribution of Tony Oxley's to drum/percussion playing, but I needed more regard for the specific sustaining of certain sounds rather than a focus primarily on motion. I wanted to be able to work a single instrument in this way as a part of, for example, sustaining a line of percussive melodic development. I didn't want to be restricted by style however, and instead needed to develop a wider flexibility of grip on the sticks.

The ribbed instruments I developed—the pieces of rectangular brass and other metals, and the numerous larger cowbells I had made out of brass or aluminium—were created with this need in mind, and the technique of being able to play surfaces horizontally and tightly within a line-moving cipher of sound   became essential.

So a very humble piece of seemingly unappealing aluminium incredulously brought over from Australia offered an enormous amount of practice and research. A great musical instrument in fact!

These are two lengths of fine sprung steel found in the dusty back shelves of a drum and percussion hire company in east London long ago. The longest measures 15cms x 130cms; the shortest 15 x 85. They are rolled and held in place by two strong, short leather straps for ease of packing and transport.

Waved like a length of rope, these produce an incredible, tight mini thunder sheet with a complex roar that can be sustained effortlessly. Because of their length and dynamic, these are not sound sources that can be easily used sitting down. I cut them down to these sizes in fact, from one long length, because they would have been very difficult to manage otherwise. One has to stand in order to demonstrate their dramatic qualities, waving them about like supercharged flashes of lightning.

They are not to be bowed like slightly more rigid forms of metal might be—the musical saw, for example—being also too long to find a deserving sound. Nor are they able to be played successfully with sticks, though draped across a drumset, they can be played more as a disturbance factor to the integrity of the set, damping sonorities and allowing occasional flurries of mild electricity to burst out.

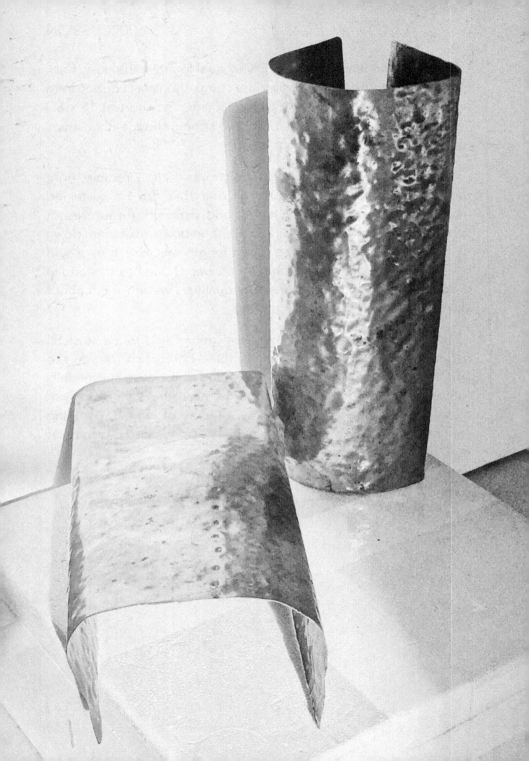

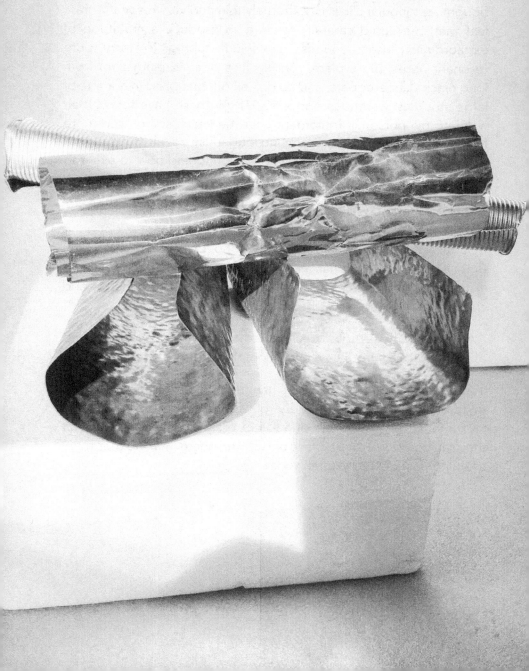

JUNK

There was a time when you could go to metal merchants here in London and get off-cuts of various metals for next to nothing. I have bought rectangular slices of extremely thin and very resonant brass leaf that one could carefully fracture to produce a multitude of extraordinary insect sounds, aluminium tubing to carry pure resonant notes, brass plate, round slices of solid aluminium from long 6inch diameter bars, and so on; all off-cuts piled in corners of large stockists' warehouses (pp. 90-91). All these have found their way into my personal equipment over the years, some used more frequently than others, and some no longer used at all. But each has helped shift my ways of thinking about sound and how to use it to create music.

These rolls of brass are no exception. They were once rectangular, but I wanted to explore the possibilities of sound that are not quite that delivered by a cowbell, and certainly not by a flat sheet of metal. Brass is a great alloy. It has a long history in the creation of musical instruments and, for percussion, has a penetrative resonance and clarity of its own, as well as being strong.

A couple of these tubes I decided to hammer to add to the tension of the metal and produce a more complex tonal quality.

Also, the indentations from the hammering left a different surface texture that enables a variety of approaches to playing the instrument. The advantage of a roll of brass like these is also that they can be placed on a surface and still resonate, making them very useful for fast dense textural work.

JUNK

These (p. 93) are four empty tins gaffa-taped together to form a set.

Of course, it is nothing new to use tins in percussion: Cage used a range of tins in his composition "Third Construction."

Mine have been well used, primarily on the floor as part of the floor set I used a lot in the very early 1980s, especially in my duo work with the singer Phil Minton. It was possible with a floor set to keep the instrumentation moving, fluidly shifting the geography of the instruments if need be, and changing the instrumentation as required without the interminable hassle of figuring out how to mount everything, which also added to the weight of the cases you would be carrying. On air travel, that is crucial. But the floor kit had two big disadvantages, the first—as has been mentioned elsewhere—being that you had to grovel on your knees in front of the audience (highly unbecoming in this day and age of style, don't you know?). And secondly, because they were placed usually directly on the floor, the instruments had limited sound projection. It was for this reason that I often used a large Flatjack bass drum as a resonating surface, one foot or so above the floor, stabilised on four legs. That really opened up the possibilities for the floor set, giving certain instruments the chance to sing out with more volume and tone.

The tin can idea I think I may have stolen from Terry Day, but I'm not sure which of us arrived at it first. I have a vague memory of Terry with tins in a cardboard box, playing at the London Musicians' Collective, but find it tricky to put a year to it. In any case, they have a limited but specific appeal and capability, being really usable and at their best with fine metal rods as beaters or perhaps the long Chinese cooks' chopsticks I favour, to get a different pitch out of each; a kind of muted gamelan effect, dry and pointillist and useful texturally or when playing melodic lines on metal. But perhaps best of all, everyone can build up a set as we all can with plastic tubs and food containers and cardboard boxes.

Often—in the right context—these things sound more interesting than an expensive drumset. No doubt one can become a connoisseur…

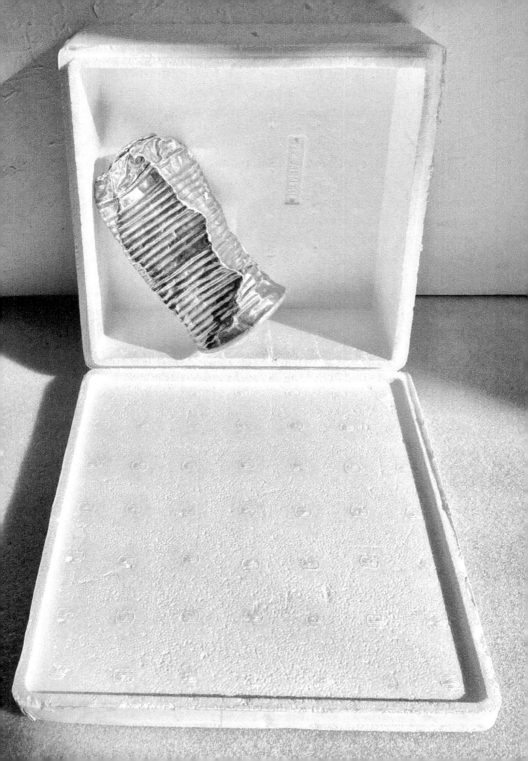

JUNK

This (pp. 96-97) is an aluminium flask I bought amongst other things from percussionist Jamie Muir when he was selling up a lot of his percussion material to focus on art-making.

I liked ribbed metal objects very much because they offer a lengthening of the sound that drummers and percussionists were only usually able to get to through playing rolls. A ribbed surface enabled the player to work with an attacking, aggressive sound, or glide over the undulations to produce a softer rolling sound or even fragment texturally with a sharper pressure on the surface. This aluminium flask was great because it resonated enough to have a certain vibrancy about it, but—a great feature of the alloy itself— was never too resonant to become as overbearing as brass can sometimes be. Also, of course, it was lightweight. This flask seems to have been hammered in various ways throughout its various incarnations, as you can see. The poor old being is badly misshapen, giving evidence to nights of outrage of one kind or another, no doubt…!

This (p. 99) is a bell from a hotel reception desk, given to me by Jock Cumming's son sometime after his father had died. Jock was a player I had known of for some time because he had been the drummer-percussionist who, in addition to playing in the Joe Loss Orchestra and then, in 1953, the BBC Show Band, also worked the Goon Show radio broadcasts with the great Wally Stott Orchestra, a programme I used to listen to for years after 1953. If ever there was a radio show that combined speed of delivery and ideas with humour and music in one amazing half hour of often creative brilliance, it was the Goon Show. And of course, sound effects were also very much to the fore throughout.

I've enjoyed using this bell for almost 30 years or so, pressing on it to ring in those occasional moments of unsteady silence during an improvisation, when musical inspiration has deserted the musicians on stage, or a lull has ensued that just needs a distasteful nudge to wake it—or myself—up. There's nothing like bad taste to remind us that music is perhaps best alive.

This bell is kept alive simply by winding it up. And you…?

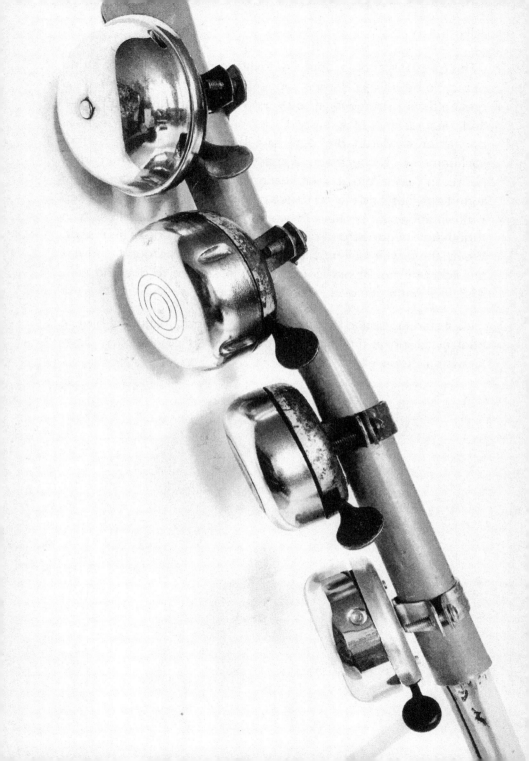

JUNK

This (p. 101) is another Jock Cummings percussive device, a string of bicycle bells fixed along a copper pipe, in pitch sequence. It's a great effects instrument—if you would ever want to use that term—and reminds me of a story I was once told by the Viennese percussionist Martin Breinschmidt about the composer Helmut Lachenmann. Lachenmann apparently went round numerous houses in Vienna late at night, testing out their doorbells for certain sound qualities, and having to flee down the road to avoid doorstep confrontations or buckets of water. He later got Martin to put together a soundboard of doorbells to be used in one of his pieces. Well… the bicycle bell pipe is much easier to carry around, and was arrived at no doubt with considerably less stress to one and all… And Jock got to it a good 40 years previously…!

It's a startling sound that one is instantly familiar with, the bicycle after all taking an important part in British musical life, as Daisy knows only too well.

JUNK

I went to Australia first in 1984 at the invitation of Jon Rose, who had put together a group of musicians that included Maggie Nichols and Jim Denley for a tour. This was an incredible time, as was what I saw and learnt of Australia. We had something like twenty-one gigs in three and a half weeks, playing in such places as Wollongong and—starkly memorable—the Cell Block in Sydney, which had been where female prisoners from the U.K. were first locked up on arrival into the country. Not high enough to stand up in, the cells' floors and ceilings were still visible striations in the block's structure. The place had a very bleak atmosphere even in 1984—*1984!*—and one couldn't help but reflect on the nature of colonisation as a means of abuse and domination, violently enforcing the rules of law of the instigating "mother" country. At that time, Australia must have increasingly felt like a cell block to its indigenous population as well as to its new arrivals.

Anyway, our itinerary took us close to where Martin Davidson of Emanem Records lived. We played a concert the day before—or was it after?—and visited Martin, who invited me into a room in his home in which he had constructed a circle of percussion— suspended cymbal trees, pieces of refrigerators or washing machines, kitchen and office stuff, all assembled and mostly suspended from frames amongst drums big and small. Martin reminded me: "We were living in Sydney in the inner-suburb of Redfern. I have no idea where I acquired the various objects, except they were mostly found in America or Australia." You had to step inside the arena and prepare to be bamboozled.

I don't know whether he brought the lot over with him when he moved back to the U.K, but he got in touch at some point and very generously gave me some bits of special "junk" and some modified old cymbals to add to my own heaps of material. Amongst these was this memorable over-size metal tray (p. 103), complete with the holes he had drilled to suspend it. I can't say that it went out to work that often, part of the problem with "junk percussion" being its portability, and as we have said often enough, especially with air travel and the economics involved. But I nevertheless often used it on the floor as part of my floor kit, and could use it as a tray is used, to put things on and move around—a kind of sound-offerings joke for the audience—and of course, use it as a sound source in its own right.

As mentioned elsewhere, the flexibilities of a floor kit enabled the shifting of individual instruments as the music develops, forming zones of pitch or texture, even shape likeness or not, that can be re-assembled or added to. Indeed, the visual quality of the player alone could enhance or even conduct decisions. It was a practical way also of circumventing the issue of mounting each percussive object/instrument and totally abolishing the need, therefore, of carrying stands and setting everything up—and then the horror of having to pack it all up meticulously after, remembering what went where. The private nightmares of the drummer/percussionist could multiply alarmingly, and the floor kit was a way of enhancing fluidity whilst reducing aggravation.

All those musical flexibilities are largely lost with a fixed-frame or fixed-form percussion set-up, no matter how expansive it might be. The only way to readily combat this problem of fixity in a drumset or percussion set-up is to use the actual drum surfaces themselves as floors for instrument placement and grouping. The drumheads can then act as resonant surfaces, though this can be a mixed blessing: size limitations combined with the specific properties of sound capability can have their issues. Working on a percussion instrument in this way, however, can develop one's ear and hand techniques— for example in this instance, the variations of sound according to how a percussion instrument is placed on the drumhead and how it is then played, is a large part of what technique is.

The tray has a kind of trash thunder quality to it, and of course, can be scraped and played like a metal-headed drum. A heavy metal, metal-headed drum. But it needn't be.

JUNK

These (p. 107) are in fact two brass beauties that I used to play a lot. I found them in the late 1970s or very early 80s in my local street market, just as they are now: two long, 20cm wide, brass sheets with three folds for the shortest, and four for the longest, which measures 175cm in length. They can be fixed onto a cymbal stand with the horizontal plane of one section drilled for an accommodating hole, and the rest shaped outwards and upwards like the wings of a large bird. The amazing thing is that the Wings can be folded up to be carried in a case and unfolded to be played, yet have never shown any signs of cracking along any of the folds. They feel very malleable, and I used to be able to curl at least one of them folded around the inside of a bass drum case, often around the red sparkle Meazzi pedal tom-tom I frequently used alongside them. That way they could protect each other.

They have a very special sound quality, whether bowed to give a wide range of sometimes searing frequencies, slid over repeatedly by thin steel rods or sticks, or played as gong surfaces with beaters or sticks. One might imagine them featuring in something like Penderecki's incredible "Threnody," such is their scope for dark messages. Having had them for a long time, they inspired me to hunt for means of electronic sound manipulation, octave dividing, and ways to open up their range even further. At the time, octave dividers couldn't handle the frequencies of a cymbal or indeed a brass sheet. After long consultations with Hugh Davies and Philipp Wachsmann around the subjects of stress gauges for bridges and all kinds of stuff that very nearly managed to put me off the notion totally, I came across an EMS Synthi A that I used for a year or two on occasion, putting a bug on the Wing and feeding it through the ring modulators. After a couple of dozen gigs with the Recedents (a long-standing electro-acoustic trio with Lol Coxhill and Mike Cooper), the nightmare of plugs and wires and knobs and patch boards finally managed to scare me off electronics I hope for life, and the Synthi A was dutifully sold to Thomas Lehn, who persuaded it into proper behaviour.

Is there a term in contemporary percussion composition for "slid over repeatedly," or is it more an instruction for an assisted Japanese bath? Whichever, the Wings have been caressed for many years by something like a long metal needle or my old double-bass bow, under my watchful eye and ear.

They have also travelled with me quite a lot, and in the early days of their life went with me cunningly disguised—being wrapped in newspaper—across the Atlantic on Virgin Air into Newark airport, U.S.A. At customs, where I was so nervous of entry interrogations, having been hitherto advised by Chris Cutler to even post my drumsticks in advance, I was wearing a suit that looked presentable from the waist up. I had been also advised to wear a suit as a tactic of true-Brit formidable self-representation. I remember it carried some of that stylistic inscrutability in the upper, frontline jacket section, but fell short in the lower rhythm section department of the trousers.

However, the customs baggage searcher was more interested in my old Gorgonzola cheese sandwich, the very early Virgin flights having suggested we provide our own food (or am I imagining this?).

The cheese sandwich, more than the totality of me, the suit variations, my percussion variations, and my brass sound-sheets, became the primary suspect intruding into U.S.A. territory.

My dear old brass sheets, somehow redolent of archaic or medieval forms of combat or some ancient otherworldliness, were clearly not an issue. Wrapped up in newspaper and string, and presented by someone in a seriously out-of-date, suspicious suit, the Wings added stature to my grand entry and I was firmly declared a product of the wilful British eccentricity so beloved by Americans, and so was strangely welcomed into the voluminous bosom of the U.S.A. without any further fuss.

I think I probably took the Wings with me—or at least the longest one—when I first went to the States at the invitation of Jack Wright. I knew nothing of Jack, but later during the visit had the dubious fortune to travel with him between New York and Minneapolis in his infamous Dodge Dart, with its half-missing floor below your feet, and encrustations of glutinous fruit that dropped year on year from the trees in the street he parked the car on, gradually changing its outward shape above. The buffalo stopped grazing in wonderment and awe as we whizzed by, throwing them peanuts to perk up lunch. The long road to the deep north indeed.

So, I've had the brass sheets since 1983 at least, and I can report that they have been very useful indeed. They last surfaced at the Sage Theatre in Newcastle with Phil Minton and Ute Wasserman, when, for a project in celebration of Kurt Schwitters, their non-regulation shape and sound spectrum lent the kind of quality the situation demanded.

Difficult, but not impossible then to travel with, and certainly worth the effort when you consider that the Wings can be easily mounted on a wide-based cymbal stand. Whether being bowed or scraped with metal implements like forks, or played gong-like, the possible movement of the Wings gave a special oscillating resonance to the sound.

Great instruments, with a very wide sound potential.

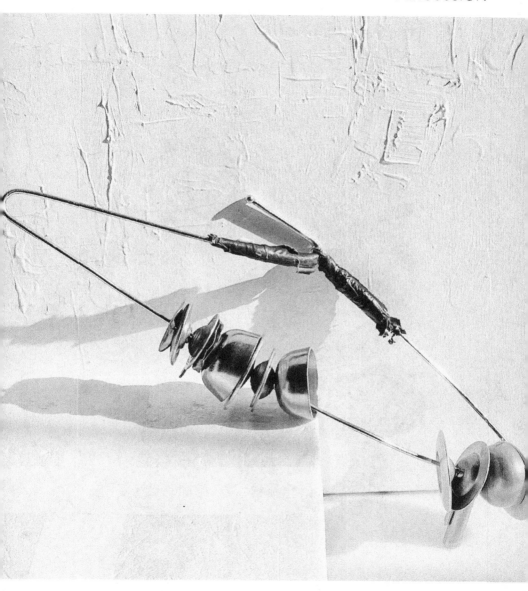

JUNK

In their Handbook of Percussion Instruments, Karl Peinkofer and Fritz Tannigel tell us that:

> Today's percussionist faces the problem of having to elicit from all sorts of different rattle instruments precisely notated beats and series of beats, which have to be performed in an exact manner, i.e., in the 'finer rhythm,' as [Curt] Sachs calls it. This demands absolute precision in starting and stopping the rattle sounds, which can only be achieved through skilful manipulation, adapted to whichever rattle is used at any given moment.[13]

No doubt this is all true, however unpalatable it might seem, but one thing as a purveyor of both the finer and not so fine rhythms, is that rattles and shakers seemed at least the easiest things for a percussionist to make. Find a container, fill it with some rattly stuff––rice, ball bearings, scraps of metal, seeds, bones, teeth etc—and shake it. Easy, and these self-made varieties are invariably more interesting consequently than those bought from a shop—a rule, I would suggest, which can be applied to most percussion. In a world where everything makes a sound, shop-bought, business-designed percussion seems like a missed opportunity—this, of course, apart from tuned percussion and maybe members of the gong family... and maybe some etceteras...

You can no doubt think of one or two others, but fundamentally I'm talking about the invention of sound -sources existing outside the domain offered by the industry and the needs of appointed musics. Small cardboard boxes, aluminium or plastic tubes, lengths of wire strung with all manner of small objects, and so on, can all house percussive rattles and shakers.

JUNK

Percussionists can invent sounds—this is the thing—and thereby invent the instrument that produces them. And/or vice-versa...

p. 111

And so to the coat-hanger rattle.

I remember I had a lot of very small finger cymbals, cheap bits of tambourine-type, pressed-out discs, fragments of old cymbals— cut-outs from cracked cymbal repairs, some with rivet-holes in them—and then lots of door keys. Metals of different alloys and densities like that. I decided to string them on an old wire coat-hanger, the simple sort you get from dry-cleaners or pound shops. It makes it possible to shake the lot, or control what you choose to allow to rattle. This creates a great sound, not too sweet and wind-chime-y, and—very important—it's easy to pack and not too heavy. Plus, being so easy to make oneself, it can be personalised with all kinds of found or self-made shaky things—cardboard rattles—why not ?—for that dry, thank-god-you're-not-here kind of ambience, or a long-hunted-for collection of stones-with-holes strung up for that rare musical moment when the ocean sweeps the pebbled beach, late at night, when you're feeling like the hippy you hoped you never were, or alone in the universe... naked to the world... etc., etc.... etc.

Incidentally, almost talking about trousers reminds me that I very much like the idea of small, portable—the males amongst us could almost say—"pocket" percussion... Things that one can carry easily and that can create an interesting sound. Which comes close to reminding me in turn of a situation I found myself in long ago in the days of the London Musicians' Collective, when a small festival celebrating the collective was taking place. Things spilled over into the street outside, and I remember standing in the drizzle with Steve Beresford and Alvin Lucier as Alvin was being interviewed, and it was suggested that Beresforth and I accompany him. Well, Steve produced a minute plastic harmonica from his jacket pocket, as he was prone to do, and all I could find—aah, those were the days— were a couple of pound notes and some small change. Live money! Whilst Steve was struggling not to swallow the harmonica, giving new definition to the term "mouth organ," which in turn might provoke the need for a moniker for a new variant further south in the downstairs department—might it be "harsmonica," a term, no doubt, some French might render a little more explicit with their quaint pronunciation preferences. So, whilst this was going on, I was struggling to make money finally musical in my damp and grubby paws, crinkling pound notes and juggling coins to provide a scintillatingly subtle backdrop for Steve's riveting solo virtuosics and Alvin's oral declarations and pronouncements... Pocket percussion indeed! We should be millionaires... or asked to quietly leave...

Is there no end to it? Percussion abounds. Perhaps I should simply have stuck a microphone in the vicinity of my recedent head and amplified the raindrops falling. Do we have a performance piece here, did someone just ask? An arena where music, art, and ritual can join? The Hair-free Orchestra performs "Standing in the Rain... Again," bringing you a million novel sounds. After all, it's extremely likely, as both classically trained singers and the Tantrics and Buddhists of Tibet have no doubt an awareness of, that each of our skulls is tuned differently... no? It could almost be a unique, deep musical experience... Ecological music (perhaps the theme of this book, in fact)...

"Preposterous! I don't wish to know that... Kindly leave the stage," came the reply.

JUNK

Anyway, let's look at some of these instruments separately, because their specificities in a sense demand it:

p. 112

This is a shaker made up with an interesting mix of bells and pieces taken from broken cymbals. I spent quite a lot of time in Tokyo hunting for a set of Ekiro used in Kabuki because they give a really full-on jangly sound. Ekiro are essentially bronze bells in the form of a hollow ring with a circumferential slot on the outside. Inside the ring, a stone or bronze ball is placed to convert the bell into a kind of rattle rather than the conventional western bell. The Kabuki Ekiro have three such bells of different sizes and weights, strung on a semi-circular frame with a handle across the flat top section. They are extremely loud, and I came to the conclusion that they were perhaps too loud and strident for most of my purposes. Luckily, when Mari and I were walking round the Tomioka Hachimangu antique "street" market in Tokyo one day, we found three old Ekiro of a thinner, more worn bronze, and far cheaper than the formal Kabuki Ekiro I had bought. Suiting my needs better, I strung these on some wire with a couple of fragments of bronze I had smoothed out, cut from a badly cracked old Zildjian I had lying around for a long time. These plus a small bell from somewhere or other gave a more rattling, less penetrative sound than the heavier gauge Ekiro set I already had.

For a percussionist, street markets can be a slice of pure magic, opening up all kinds of possibilities. Never knowing what you may find, they can offer a range from the world of chance that none of the stocked preconceptions of a music shop can cover.

We are indeed in rattle mode, and not just because we are all getting older. The inclusion of all these instruments in one section belies the fact that they are in many ways quite different instruments in their own right. They are all rattles and shakers, but this instrument—returning to the coat-hanger rattle—has features of its own that make it even more specific and special.

Apart from the fact that there are door keys, telephone bells, finger cymbals of different sizes, and a couple of tambourine jingles, all strung on a wire dry-cleaner's coat hanger, this is an instrument of quality that can really be played. I can use it as a kind of brush to glide over the surface of drums, with or without metal instruments placed on top, giving a more sonorous jangle than a chain would create, but equally able to summon up sheer noise if needed. Or I can hold it carefully and separate certain pieces to control the pitch or textural quality of the sounds produced, giving an accurate dryness to space that can be supported by very small sounds, maintained or clearly separate. The shaker can then, of course, be properly shaken to produce a wall of sound that can be layered into other stuff going on, or provide a landscape of sound for other instruments to build their story on top.

p. 113

These are shakers from yet another dimension, giving a kind of firm but ethereal lightness, not sweet in the annoying way that suspended sets of chimes can be—making you wish for a conceptual brick to throw at the music—but robustly, metallically light...

And so they should be. These shakers were put together by the great Max Lewin, who played with Fats Waller on the six tracks that made up the London Suite, recorded in 1939. Despite the suggestion according to George Burrows that "an investigation of Waller's suite suggests a way of listening to the effects of transatlanticism in music that takes account of the social politics that are bound up with it,"[14] one can barely hear Max, so discreet was he in his accompaniment of Mr. Waller. But his presence is felt much as his two sets of shakers can be felt rather than heard, if you so wish.

Max was a generous soul, and gave me these along with some other very wonderful drums and percussion instruments that include a 2.5 octave Honduras Rosewood xylophone fitted onto a portable wooden base, the brass badge on which declares:

Tuned Percussion
Frederick Close
London W2

I believe it was a Besson product, Frederick Close being one of their addresses in London and previously a factory for Besson's mouth-organ production.

Max must have collected the small, fine metal discs for these two shakers over a period of time, the more densely packed shaker giving more charge than its companion, which conducts its spirit more politely.

To sustain the legend, Max also told me that Fats Waller had a large bottle of whisky sitting on the piano—confirmed, in fact, by Burrows also. Hopefully he was taking full advantage of the pleasures of life in the U.K., feeding them into his incredible musicality with such fervent grace and wit. I never thought to ask if he shared it all with Max...

p. 114

I put this instrument together from an array of quite heavy small cymbals, both bronze and nickel silver. It's not really a shaker because I wanted an instrument that was more physically flexible, so that I could bunch the cymbals up to alter their sound, and for this reason strung them on a strong cord. Very simple indeed, but nevertheless an instrument I use a lot, often having it sit on a drum head to strike or push with a stick as a kind of grace-note texture underpinning more prominent sounds and strikes. More pronouncedly resonant than the shakers, it can also be juggled in one hand to give a continuum of sound. I like this a lot: finding instruments that offer a variety of possibilities. Plus, it helps in the battle with weight, transport, costs, health... etc., etc.

p. 115

Extending the tonal panorama of rattles and shakers, I made this instrument because I wanted to find a sound that had the quality of bubbles colliding, something clear and definite but also somehow with air and buoyancy. "Are you mad ?" asked the Conservative Party Minister for Culture and Corruption one day. Well, I'll dodge that question and simply say I had a bag of ping-pong balls sitting around doing nothing—as they often do—so put a hole through a few and strung them along a wire coat-hanger, curved the hanger so that I could shake it like a hammer, and thought it would survive a few seconds occasionally at some point in a very low volume concert. It really does have a place, but looks kind of daft enough to every now and then get a few laughs from an audience. Strange to say, it also demanded a playing action that always made me think of

JUNK

the knife-in-the-shower scene in Psycho... well, there have been a few musicians down the road I could relish swatting with a few nouns and adjectives, but really... ping-pong balls and a coathanger... I could have been arrested!

p. 116

This is a small box with a variety of shakers inside, the sort that are relatively easy to make oneself, and often far more interesting than shop-bought equivalents—the plastic egg filled with seed variety, for example. Amongst these are plastic and aluminium tubes that were probably used for lozenges of different kinds, and contain whatever rattling materials you have to hand that sound the way you want them to sound—seeds, rice, ball bearings, nails, nuts, etc. One or two of these have a small piece of probably calf skin from an old drumhead stretched and glued over so that the shaker can create a different kind of sound. One is made from an old linseed oil tin I had that I simply unscrewed the top from, cleaned out, and then put a couple of ball bearings inside... and then screwed the top back. Things like that. Then you shake them, whenever and wherever you like...social gatherings, political rallies, chatting to your in-laws, anywhere where a little light percussion can add colour and depth. You will become the heart and soul of gatherings everywhere. Even music events.

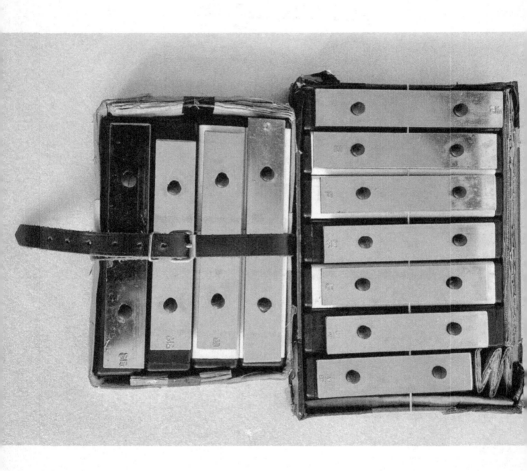

This first photo (p. 125) is the very wonderful Pixiphone xylophone, produced for children and with the note-bars in great colours. The next photo (p. 126) is of two instruments with a similar approach—trying to get compact melodic instruments that are easy to carry and practical to set up in mid-concert.

The Pixiphone I found in the Portobello Market in London was cheap and alluring. It's such a nice thing to have! To be able to inject clearly pitched notes into a drum-based or even percussion-based set is a tricky thing. Weight and size issues abound, but obviously these instruments are not going to have the scope, volume, or quality of note that a full set of vibes or even a glockenspiel would provide. No matter. What they provide for me is what I can call a "pitch texture," something, no matter how limited, that offers a note or pitch that can allow or suggest the construction of a texture. Alternatively, a single, clear pitched note can sometimes offer a contrast within the music surrounding it, creating effective punctuation or offering signposts for the immediate future musical direction during improvisations.

Using the Pixiphone to summon up vestiges of western musical culture—it has an approximate tuned octave after all—provokes a kind of inverted musical deceit, the sound from one bar perhaps showing up the base iniquities of percussion sounds coming from chains and forks scraping over kitchen utensils. "Remember your musical traditions," it is saying! Joking aside—almost—these small metallophones are an absolute delight. I love the ones I have arranged in small re-enforced cardboard boxes that can be re-arranged entirely if I choose, vibrant full notes sounding out in simple patterns or rattled with sticks of various sorts. They stand out, reminding us of tradition indeed, and with the Pixiphone, also the blithe fun of child-play before instructions set in.

JUNK

I used to use more toys at one point—long ago in the late 1970s—though never to the extent of Martin Klapper, whose range and dexterity in the use of all kinds of toys to create musical landscapes is miraculous. But I found their use didn't weigh with my needs to still somehow play the drums, even if I was often using pieces of old metal to do it on. And the truth of it is, you can only carry so much stuff to the concert, unless, of course, you are another person, in which case you employ your own private convoy of lorries, and perhaps don't really need to read this book at all.

JUNK

There was a time, as I have just mentioned, when I used toys more often, but somehow I kind of grew out of it…

Anyway… this is an old space gun (p. 129) I found somewhere, probably when I used to hang out with Darth and a few of his buddies: The Dark Faders, as my daughter Dixie would call them when a tot.

Well, what to say? You press the trigger, and it coughs out a kind of whirring sound that can be useful once in a while; and it also gives off a red glow at the same time to show it's embarrassed at being taken seriously. (Reconstructed "assault" gun…)

Have you got one?… Martin Klapper has seventeen…tuned.

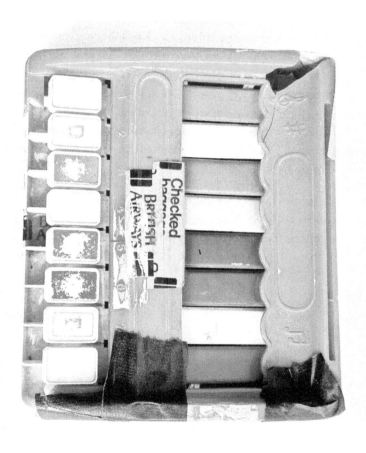

JUNK

This (p. 131) is a very young child's toy piano found in a market somewhere in London a long time ago. It has a very tinny sound that I like and has proved very useful both as a kind of punctuator and for weird melodic rambles.

Unfortunately, over the years it has suffered certain damage, getting packed too hastily perhaps and half crushed in suitcases as air cargo. As usual, my trusty medic in all these matters—gaffa tape——has solved the problem of cracks in the plastic casing and helped toughen it up for future journeys. Maybe we can also recognise a little British Air tape I scrounged at a check-in once and used to support the instrument when it was in dire straits. I have a strong liking for sticky tape of all kinds, always hunting in my all-time favourite shop, Tokyo Hands, for rolls of gaffa and other tapes, or trying to cadge tape from the check-in counters of airports everywhere.

I remember this piano was heavily featured during recordings made with Mr. Klapper for the "Recent Croaks" album we recorded in Prague long ago. Quite right, too.

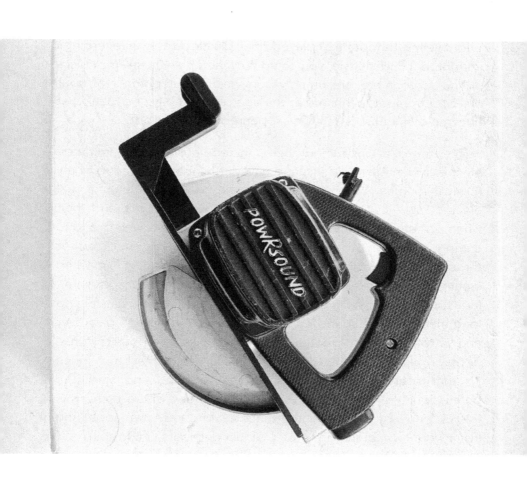

JUNK

Really letting things down here, I have to confess to buying this in a shop. Not only a shop, but one right in the very heart of London— the children's toyshop, Hamley's, on Regent Street.

Further confessions would reveal it (p. 133) to be not the only thing I've bought there that I have used for music. I once had a fantastic bright yellow trumpet that played small plastic discs with recordings imprinted, LP vinyl-style; you could blow and play these small discs at the same time, presumably convincing your parents of your amazing trumpet technique at the age of four. I have no idea what became of it, but it certainly disappeared from my sight...

This particular instrument here, incredulously, is an imitation electric saw made of plastic, and I used it a lot at one period of my musical journey. When you pull the string—like with an actual electric saw—it starts a particular frictional saw sound, and then when something is put in the way of the plastic saw wheel, a loud cutting sound is produced. Excellent for sending shock waves through a misbehaving band on stage, but very useful, in fact, when creating dense textural material of the urban soundscape, semi-industrial type. Again, it especially proved its value when sustaining long machine-type sounds. It made it possible for me to play over and with this sustain, creating dense passages of various textures, or playing lines over the top of it. Seriously useful, maybe so much so that every percussionist should have one... not just the percussionist or drummer, every band member, entire orchestras even... and why not? Hear the Electric Saw Orchestra, appearing live in your local orchard... etc.... Or just get yourself a lyrebird.

JUNK

What we have here (p. 135) are two quite large round bells as used in the decorative percussion-dressing of certain elephants in parts of India. These, however, I found in my local market from a dealer who had just returned from India and was selling his wares to one and all. How he could travel with such heavy objects amongst the many others I have no idea. Certainly, he wasn't a blithe hippy coming back with a few joss sticks and a tiny brass Buddha. This man was in business, and really I shouldn't perhaps have bought them at all. So, in a sense, they are and are not junk instruments, their original purpose and beauty being somewhat tainted by the touch of business and profit.

It's a tricky thing: the theft of another country's culture and artefacts by the west. It's that colonial, capitalist, entrepreneurial greed that desecrates some places and cultures, and—of course—ourselves in the process…

Well, what to do?

Of course, I bought them, sitting there on a table looking suitably exotic and mystifying. It was probably grey and raining, and I could hear the trinkle-tinkle of the far-away.

Well… from the racket they can make when I got hold of them, especially now that I joined them as a pair that can be held in one hand and shaken, I am very glad that I did. They produce a scary roar, jangling the nerves and upsetting everyone. Of course, an elephant plays them with far more delicacy and aplomb, shimmying on its way while the drums are beaten around it…

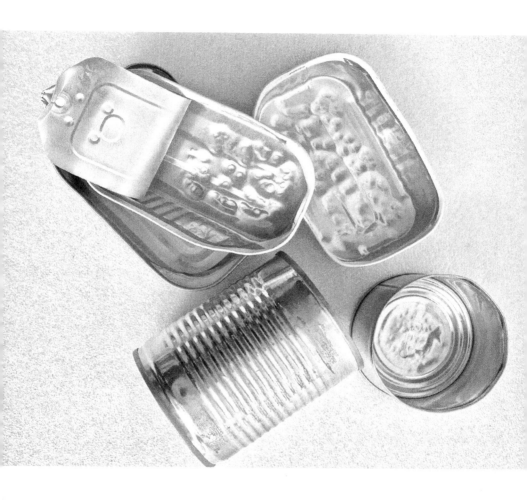

JUNK

This collection of small opened tins and metal bowls (p. 137) makes a very simple percussion tool, useful for manipulating as a disassembled rattle or for playing lightly with fine metal rods or needles. The thing I like about these is the dulled, flattened tonality, giving them a dry clarity that can be very fertile in certain musical situations. More useful, therefore, in intimate musical settings, or indeed whilst recording.

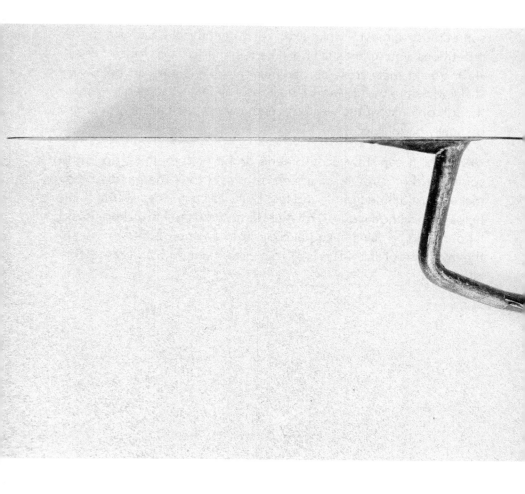

JUNK

A plasterer's trowel (p. 139), and the best one I ever saw or heard. I begged it from dear old Gionni Gardini (who, at the time, ran the Area Sismica outside Forli in Italy) because its blade was broad but thin and finely tempered with almost sharp edges. I knew it would make a great sound. I play it almost always with my short German double-bass bow and have used it very often to provide something sometimes almost violin-like, or rhythmically constant, or repetitious, you might still find in certain musics from Africa or Asia. Having said that, cross-border musical pollination can be a very sticky wicket to tread—world music and all that western glue—even though defence of the western-centric word "ethnic" may seem to be finally dissolving.

Anyway, it can offer up the eerie drone or something up in the spirit-world of carefully-sourced ecstasies. I took the handle off to make it just a little lighter and less bulky to carry—every little thing helps in this endeavour—and it, in turn, seems to have shed its old labours and remains naked and open to any new attention. Aaah, the mysteries of life… This is a great instrument, with a vibrant clarity all its own.

JUNK

This (p. 141) is beautiful. It came from a London hospital, and was given to me by a member of the audience at a Mopomoso night at the Vortex in London. I wondered if it had been used to comb straight the intestines of disorderly patients, perhaps tuning them ready for the surgeon to strum in the operating theatre. It's quite light but very solid, and being made from aluminium, rings with a less painful sustain than some brass objects might do. Aluminium is the percussionists' best-kept secret; a less obvious sound-making alloy than brass, its nature carries less obligation to ring out with any stridency, giving a slightly soapy roundness to its tones.

I love this instrument. It's easy to pack, relatively light, catches the eye with its design, and offers a range of possible ways it can be played. It can be struck with a stick quite forcefully or—indeed, *struck*—or rubbed such that each tooth or tine is sounded, producing slightly different pitches and a waterfall of sounds. And it can also be used as a friction instrument over a drumhead treated with rosin to give grip, creating a really sharp yet melodious attack. I have also used it against the edge of a spinning cymbal, which can produce a kind of ethereal airscape, something that rays of sunshine might sound like, if only they could.

JUNK

The forks (p. 143) are a long-term favourite item of mine, and I almost never play a gig or a concert without them in my stick bag. Again, the goal of their inception was primarily to increase the possibility to sustain a sound over a period of time without having to resort to the hand-to-hand drum roll technique.

Of course, using the forks also opened up textural sound possibilities. I found that if I rubbed the surface of a drum with violin players' rosin, I was able to get extra friction on the surface, making the forks a really strong sound source. Naturally, one has to be extremely careful doing this: one is not jabbing a steak. Puncturing the drumhead or wearing it excessively thin is not what you want to be doing, so extra caution is the name of the game in this department.

I have been using plastic forks taped together for a long time, and use these mainly on a drumhead to create a rasping, guttural sound that can be either delivered as punctuation or extended into a long paper-ripping sound. I also use a regular dining fork on metal surfaces—on the Wings, on brass plates, even lightly on cymbals if it felt suitable. I most recently find myself using it with the utmost care on a rosined floor tom's head to produce a complex, somewhat ethereal multi-glissandi effect.

This particular fork is also a great instrument in itself. No doubt a very particular alloy! Placed on a bed of foam rubber and struck with a thin metal needle, it can produce a very distinct note, extremely useful in certain precise contexts, and has even been known to draw smiles of approval from members of the audience, I am told. So much for attention-seeking antics.

It goes without saying—and indeed why this is not common knowledge is difficult to comprehend—that percussively some plastic and regular metal forks are better to use than others. For sure you need a strong, relatively inflexible plastic fork, and a dining fork also with a quality tine. Of the latter, the one I am currently using I found in a shop selling all kinds of second-hand goods, somewhere on the road in the midwest when Konk Pack were touring in the U.S.A. We had stopped for a breather, spotted the shop, and went in. The band was always looking out for cheap American clothing of a certain style—whatever the hell that was. Probably gaberdine suits and country and western shirts... or just cheap jeans, or almost anything else, anything, that is, that would stop us having to go into horrendous clothes shops in London or Vienna, where loud manufactured music designed to remove brain cells permanently is played. Do... you... know... what I mean? Well... I came away with a fork. So there you are. It had "ROGERS" stamped into it as the maker's mark, so I had to have it. I've never got round to scratching in the apostrophe, but it's been the best fork I've had... although—while we are on the topic—I feel compelled to tell you, dear reader, that I did get a top quality Parisian fork in the Portobello Road Market one day... Aaah yes, madam, I am what is called a connoisseur, don't you know... ahem...

So... a good fork is clearly something to behold, an object of many functions...

This actually isn't a homemade or found piece of equipment but has so many interesting qualities that step outside the notions of conventional percussion that it would somehow qualify for most categories within that family. It is an instrument that was manufactured in small quantities by the Ludwig Drum Company (featured in their 1927 catalogue as the 'Ludwig Gladstone Cymbal'), and then by the Leedy Drum Company in the following year, both after a design by Billy Gladstone, the New York Radio City Music Hall percussionist and inventor. Essentially, it is a hand-held device for squeezing—clashing or clanging—two cymbals together: in effect, a hand-held hi-hat.

The Leedy catalogue of that year tells us, "they can be made to produce a world of varied effects in straight or syncopated rhythms. Will either 'ring' or 'sock.'"

Interestingly, both this description and the name given to these Gladstone cymbals' forerunner—the Leedy Bock-a-da-Bock cymbals—stand as evidence for percussion's great merit as individual instruments beyond ready classification or indeed commodification, and stand definable, in many instances, solely by onomatopoeia. Tom-tom? Pang cymbal? Swish cymbal?

(Are other instruments like this? It is tricky to think of the violin in this way, though, of course the name itself has been used metaphorically, which might count: "Love is like a violin…"

Perhaps, yet doubtless not one played by Sherlock Holmes, with a sound designed to shred Dr. Watson's brain. Aaah, but wait. . . The second line: "with its strings around your heart…")

Looking at it closely, there is something about this "hand, sock cymbal" that has the qualities of the beautifully bizarre about it that justifies its inclusion here. Even though carefully thought out, it nevertheless retains a kind of Heath Robinson spontaneity to its springs and coal-tongs structure, with rivets clamping the cymbals in place. Very beautiful, and this bizarre mix of design and manufacture is carried through into the instrument's actual sound, which is far removed from the ringing sustain of small heavy Chinese cymbals or of most cymbals we would think of. These instead are choked, dry, and very much an acquired taste.

Percussionists of the time, as we read in the introduction, were familiar with the need to invent sounds, and so this instrument, reclaiming the traditional use of cymbals as instruments to be played in pairs only, gained a place in their arsenal as a forerunner of the conventional, foot-operated hi-hat pedal. Small, light, and compact, they were easy to carry, and could be played with great intricacy—hear Chick Webb with the Jungle Band play his on "Dog Bottom," or Kaiser Marshall with Fletcher Henderson & His Orchestra: "Whiteman Stomp" in May 1927.

I have to be careful using my set of these: they are not so strong that one can be reckless in playing them or in travelling with them, and so they have appeared infrequently but to special effect, fitting well into the array of instruments I can use with perhaps greater freedom.

Most importantly, however, they also serve to remind us how vocabularies expand in the world of percussion and can be recognised by manufacturers with a good ear. Are those days passed now that the computer has taken over? Surely the percussionists' world, in which everything has a sound, can transcend such a danger and simply subsume the computer into its vocabulary should it choose to…

One of the main materials the planet throws away and now tries hard to hopefully recycle and reconsider its strategies about is paper. But paper can also be great sonic detritus—cardboard too—and, of course, it is light and easy to transport in small quantities.

Paper can provide clouds of sound or crisp detail depending on its type. It can crackle and pop, swish and sway like the wind itself, and so provides a great instrument for the percussionist to use in very special musical situations.

The last time I used paper in a full-on sonic way was at the White Cube Art Gallery in London, where Christian Marclay had organised a series for soloists to play in conjunction with his exhibition there. We were all offered an evocative brief by Christian that drew on sounds from empty late-night streets, for me a perfect sonic location for all manner of junk—paper, cardboard, glass, metals, wood... liquids...

Amongst other things—the Wings featured, as, of course, did my dear old Meazzi pedal tom—I decided to take a box full of various types of paper, each with distinct sound properties.

I have been using paper percussively on occasion since the 1970s and remember very well the first time I played in Belgium, in this instance with the saxophonist Gary Todd. We had decided to catch the ferry to Calais or Boulogne and drive up to Belgium to cut across to Brussels. At the time, it seemed the quickest way.

Pretty much as soon as we had crossed the border into Belgium on a relatively quiet country road, angling our way to Brussels, we were pulled over by a police car and asked to get out. I was also asked to empty the contents of my drum cases.

JUNK

It was a beautiful sight. Spread out in the road behind us were a collection of drums that would have included small Chinese drums with their pig skins patterned by ferocious colourful dragons; western drumset drums glinting with chrome; woodblocks and one or two temple blocks, red, gold, and black; lengths of metal—brass, tin, aluminium—bits of stands and fittings to mount much of it, but most memorably, masses of different kinds of paper of different lengths, colours, and qualities. There were crumpled foils in silver and gold, and rectangles of silver paper, mirror-like; a dozen or more different kinds of poly-bags, with supermarket and specialist shop labels in various languages, winking at us all, some filled with polystyrene packing-beans blowing around, escaping into the air; gift-wrappers scrunched or rolled; all kinds of papers and foils, most very thin and chosen for their sound.

The important thing also was that the sun was shining, but it was a really windy day. The paper was performing, blowing up in festoons of waves and the poly-bags filling with air, swirling and trying to get airborne; the foils crinkling and complaining; the odd sheets of whatever paper, blowing up into the air and chasing each other, stuff glinting and rustling and bustling around. It was an unimaginable display of paper sound and visuals, absolutely surreal and fantastic. The two policemen stood staring at the action dumbfounded, wondering what on earth was going on. Why would anyone on the planet travel with all this kind of stuff? What was going on? Where was the swag? "We are musicians playing a concert tomorrow at the Palais des Beaux Arts in Brussels," we declared. "This is all percussion," I added, waving my arm around generously to include the fields and trees. "Just listen," hoping they would shut up and do just that, so that we could be on our way.

And who knows? Maybe that five minute free, but involuntary, concert on a country road in Belgium turned the local constabulary into avid sound explorers and adventurous music listeners. Knitting needles on triangles, handcuffs rattling bars with fresh aplomb: concerts for the various inmates. Worse things have happened.

JUNK

EPILOGUE

Part 1

My father had good hands. He could make things and transform existing things. Between the wars he tired of his AJS motorbike and built his own sports car, and later built two large garden sheds after the family moved up to the house my grandmother rented, and built the big workbench in one of them. He built the chicken house, too, and the big dining table and chairs, stained dark to look like ebony. And he repaired our shoes and refitted the soles when needed. He knew how to make catapults and respect and sharpen knives; how to carve and peel shapes from the bark of freshly cut ash wands; and how to flick a hockey ball with tight ferocity with a hockey stick, the way the Indian players did in the foothills of the Himalayas when he was there pre WW2. He was a country boy who knew how to live off his wits, and for me, living in Whitstable with the fields and woodland just over the road, having a stick in my hand was as natural as holding a knife and fork.

My mother, I could say, seemed a hard-working, feisty woman, but more neighbourly than my father. She would sing Arabic songs in the kitchen from time to time, reminding her own mother later, no doubt, of the time their family was in Jerusalem, where my mother was brought up. She must have inevitably been part of the British elite there, but from an unsettled background, somewhere in the

154

labyrinthine struggles between working class and the new middle classes, her father having been in the unfortunate and imperialist ranks of the Palestine Police.

Nevertheless, her singing was doubtless my first connection with live music, the cadences and particular diction being riveting for a young kid growing up in the hardships of a council estate in 1950s England. She had an energy and spirit for life, a certain flamboyance that would bubble over and make us all feel good. Like my father, I think she wanted her children to have fun.

So—however these things work—it was kind of inevitable that I would take to the drums, get the sticks in my hands, the brushes, enjoy those wooden shells, the sounds of the cymbals, the cowbell, the woodblock, and have a melodic ear in place as much as a rhythmic sense.

Part 2

As a means of doing, improvisation in music can offer a context very much for the individual to develop, hone and express personal creativity. But it can also offer a place for awareness to be respected within a group context. Obeyance to rules in these regards is not the thing. Awareness with a sense of the edge is perhaps the indicator. Getting the antennae focused and spotting the territory, music-making needs it all.

Culture, we might say, grows out of that interactivity between people, and between them and their environment. Of course, that environment is not a passive being, lying in wait perpetually in submission. It lives and flows and works its energies with the people combining with it.

Like percussion itself, improvisation as a way of making music seems to have an entirely natural capability to transform our environment's informational abundance. The need to combine and interact, feeding into a democratic imperative we cannot truly ignore; the position of the composer --- the need for a composer, for a composition—all need a fresh examination. New composition's intellectual bias; pop music's physical bias—all need fresh examination. The days of the insistent individual artist as a being separate and in some senses above the daily flow—the maintaining of the western mythology of creative separation—is perhaps slipping down a tired old drain of romanticism. The world needs to pull together, but not deny ourselves the right to have our own expressions and energies different from those of others. Collective output need not refuse individual input, nor need it exert authoritarian rules on what and how something is expressed. If you don't like it and don't agree, move on. Music has surely had enough of dealing with dictates. Primarily, it has to be enjoyable to make.

Percussion playing—as we have noted elsewhere—has long been a source of social cohesion and liberation, a means to mark pleasure as well as being a healing force.

In the social domain, having and playing percussion has become a tool or a vehicle for people to pull together. The drum circle as therapy; the samba band to show us how participation can be so much organised fun! And why not? Well, each to their own, but to me the existence of the drum circle in the west has been such a wasted opportunity for creative sharing and getting together. It's not just the strange embarrassment of witnessing Westerners trying to evoke some quasi-tribal connectivity, but the fact that it could be both more liberating and more involving without any of those old culture-colonising tropes. Plus that other ever-suffocating trope, the one that costs money to buy your tribal drum from an over-priced shop.

This can be changed. Allow yourself to imagine a room full of people playing on found materials, instruments that they have adapted and adopted as their own objects of affection, gathered over a period of time, perhaps from the locality, and consequently very much reflective of who they are and where they live. It's almost as though we should all have a bag or a box in a corner at home—a kind of culture composting—where we can put material we have spotted and collected that we would like to have and that we suspect will produce a sound. Creative recycling. And over time, these collections will grow and be edited as skills of both hearing and playing develop at their own speed. These unleashed energies could distil astonishing sounds, shared and sustained as is wished. Instruments could be exchanged, techniques figured out, pleasures enjoyed free from any baggage; in fact, it would be a properly "ecological process," as George Brecht might suggest.

I remember once long ago hearing a quite large herd of goats eating in a field in the south-east of the island of Majorca. Each was wearing a bell strung round the neck. It was an incredible sound, strong yet also incredibly delicate and extremely beautiful to listen to, each bell seeming slightly different in pitch. Music helps the goats focus in safety. A group of people playing objects of differing alloys, woods and plastics could create an elasticity of sound in a similar vein, but for sure more dynamic, something truly reflecting who they are on the planet. Perhaps we can draw inspiration from a herd of goats and their owner, and transpose the Eden ideal into a tough urban setting.[15]

Part 3

However, with my life still stranded as a pre-teenager in a post-war U.K. family, I knew it would never be enough to sit at the dinner table and jiggle my knife and fork round the plates and water glasses that caused my mother to always end up barking, "For God's sake, Roger, stop fidgeting!" Next door was a banjo and guitar player, and brother Tony, now living primarily in London to go to college, got himself a trombone, and New Orleans jazz was in the air. Then brother Ian, at art college in Canterbury, got a trumpet, and finally my father found the missing part to the puzzle and came up one day with an old and very beaten up light blue-painted drumset, and off we went.

With my eldest brother generally an absentee, Ian and I would play our fragile versions of old jazz numbers on our old beaten-up instruments, stepping out into our early teen years.

A weird, off -kilter little duo was born, and the groundwork for improvisation and sound was laid right there. My drumset had little in the way of convention to it. The bass drum, after various experiments, with my father even trying old parachute material he had stuffed away in the shed, had a cardboard batter head finally fixed in place. In those days in small-town south England, where would you ever find a proper drumhead, and what was that anyway? There was no one to tell us, and in any case the critique of a bass drum sounding like a cardboard box has long since been doing the rounds. I had unerringly just fabricated a prototype! The snare drum was tiny and warped, but had the snare sound; the cymbals also small, a little bent I remember, and one cracked, and conventionally somewhat dysfunctional. But who cared or even knew? For sure we had music; we had spirit and we listened and practised and loved to play.

To look after my mother's mother, my parents had decided to move the family up to her—my grandmother's—home, and in one of those ludicrous moves that defeats all understanding, my parents decided to get rid of the upright piano that stood in the cold front room. Did they really prefer to have the drums rattling around the brain cells? That act of betrayal must have sharpened my defiance because—even in damped-down post war U.K.—I was out of that door like a rocket when I hit thirteen, hunting down the old New Orleans jazz clubs in the town and neighbouring towns. I found four clubs in those three small towns of north Kent, a necessity for my energies and sanity after the sonic elations fuelled in my pre-teens by Jelly Roll Morton, Louis Armstrong, and Sidney Bechet on old 78s brought down from the razzamatazz of London to blast out on our creaking wind-up gramophone.

The sheer exotic otherness of my mother's singing, the constancy of birdsong, even of chicken chuckling away, and the sounds of the sea on the shingle beaches that fronted the town, had all put me right in line to take whatever music came my way straight into the bloodstream, no defence offered.

Thankfully, added to this strange national, post-war cocktail of youthful optimism and the grey stress of social struggle, we also had humour and the sardonic wit of British resolve, an ally helping the imagination to deal with all the issues of transience and change. England was a tough country to be in even in the mid 1950s, destruction, poverty and rationing leaving serious social scars. The

Goon Show of the later 1950s played over the BBC radio airwaves, and had an enormous impact on my sensibility as a pre-teenager. With a flow that veered from surreal narrative lunacy to scenarios challenging the logic of the world we lived in, the changes of sound and rhythm contained in that half-hour comedy show were mesmerizing. Including two first-rate music interludes , the show provided a much-needed respite from the strange slog of life in England post war. Time itself was held to ransom; politics savaged; racial stereotypes tested; and the imagination allowed to travel the globe and beyond. The Ray Ellington Quartet, Max Geldray and Wally Stott's Orchestra provided the music, almost as cut-ups, but the programme would also incorporate some astonishing displays of sound, not just isolated as effects but woven into the web of the narrative itself. The particulars of the existing English language, both as sound source and as meaning, were explored with rare perception and pleasure. The English radio voice in the 1950s especially—in fact up until relatively recently—was very much cultivated to sound like that of the well-educated and privileged upper-crust. The Goon Show tested the assumptions of what the human voice was hitherto allowed to sound like, and despite the occasional grating embarrassments that would occur, the voice was instrumental in exploring approaches to sound and its consequent impact on humour as never before. The programme made it clear: sound could shock, but it could also be extremely comical—when the context was right.

Most importantly for me, however, the Goon Show opened up musical possibilities I had never heard before and made them appear natural. Sound exploration and music became integral to each other.

Fortunately, with an older jazz-loving brother up in the capital city, records began to arrive whenever he would turn up at home.

Baby Dodds' incredible solo played on the bass drum hoop and woodblock, live on "China Boy," and Zutty Singleton's fantastic New Orleans drum repertoire on "Shimmy-sha-Wobble," with its snare drums rolls and block and cowbell phrases, transfixed me and eventually took on meanings that set me up for a search beyond the now-established jazz drumset. The music, its sounds and energies, opened me right up. We had to play.

And very soon—wham!!! like a Lord Buckley spirit—another of those life changers occurred and transformed the musical message forever again. In the space of, I don't know, maybe six months or a year at the most, brother Tony brought down from London three records with a different feel entirely from everything I had heard before: an EP of the Modern Jazz Quartet playing "Django"; a 10inch of the original Gerry Mulligan Quartet playing numbers like "Line for Lyons" and "Walking Shoes"; but finally, and most amazing of all—praise be to all that's holy—something that lifted the roof off and planted seeds for life, the Ornette Coleman Quartet's "Change of the Century" LP. That did it: "Ramblin'" changed my life. The sound of that band! A contained, acoustic dryness. Straight into the bloodstream. My brother and I would argue over a certain note in Charlie Haden's bass solo, but we knew much of that material—as we had before with Mulligan's Quartet songs—inside out.

So the incredible and ferocious power of Baby Dodds's on "China Boy" had morphed into the cymbal sound of Billy Higgins on "Ramblin'." Soon I was going up to London to hear the great visiting American jazz musicians. The Coltrane quartet with Eric Dolphy added was the first live concert I ever heard, so Elvin Jones' drumming started to occupy my senses like rays from the planets.

JUNK

But then there were the Ellington and Basie orchestras, with Sam Woodyard playing rolls on the snare drum rims and Sonny Payne doing the full showboat stick tricks, the power of acoustic jazz orchestras coming together as something I had never ever even dreamed of. So much followed, too much to list—from Thelonious Monk's Quartet to Miles with Tony Williams; Rollins at Ronnie's and Giuffre with Bley and Swallow. So much stuff for a U.K. teenager; incredibly lucky to be able to grab the chances to hear music that excited the air as you left the concert halls and filled you with total blasts of buzz and awareness: human magic in the big city.

But fizzing around with much of all this, other stuff was in the air also, and—no doubt about it—pushing the blood around. I was a teenager, out and about in the world. Life was finally beginning to happen. Girls, parties, music. After having to survive through the all teeth-and-neatness vacuity of Perry Como and Pat Boone clogging up the radio at home, and being eternally grateful for "Klactoveedsedstene" kicking off the weekly 30 minute slice of pretty much conventionalised Jazz, right round the corner came Buddy Holly and Elvis, Motown sometime and the Supremes, James Brown, even—a little later maybe—the Beatles, all drifting in and out , difficult to not be aware of in the great stampede and melee of teen life, and difficult not to have sometimes bouncing around, in and out of your head. I remember the Liverpool Sound and Cannonball Adderley's Sack o' Woe sitting comfortably next to each other the first time I hitch-hiked up north, an energised sixteen or seventeen year old, hanging out with the beat aristocracy at Manchester's Sovereign, and hearing Al Cohn and Zoot Sims at Club 43 before going up to Edinburgh. From my mother's start, I very firmly discovered that I loved songs, and all I was waiting for were The Who, Beefheart, Hendrix, and the Soft Machine.

And then finding a way to digest it all, stitch it all together, investigate, ruminate, search, improve, add and edit, and do all the etceteras of life.

Part 4

Having only two older brothers might well have squeezed me into a tight spot. The eldest, Tony, had for years been bringing musical information and inspiration home that ranged very comfortably from 78s of Johnny Dodds to LPs of Ornette Coleman. My middle brother, Ian, meanwhile was soon to be feeding me his enthusiasms from art college for artists that also covered an expanse of approaches—I remember seeing reproductions of work from Nicolas de Stael and Jackson Pollock, Ivon Hitchens and Pierre Bonnard. This was in the late 1950s and early 1960s, U.K.

The value within all this was less about the definition or formulation of creative approaches—we had no need at that point in time to touch on that—but more simply about opening up the response systems that allowed interest and inspiration to flow, and then to be able to play some music. The two disciplines were feeding each other in ways I had no idea about, even though by the early 1960s in London, visual art was turning its attention to what was becoming the pop world: the body was on display and the new environment of fashion was activated as art took inspiration from the streets.

Interestingly, Martin Gayford, in his thoroughly researched and compelling book *Modernists & Mavericks*, talks us through the sharp change in philosophical and psychological attitude that caused certain British artists to refocus their nostalgia for the past

JUNK

and start hunting down the future. What happened stands in contrast to what seemed to be going on in the world of jazz or pop music cultures, though the artists themselves seemed unconcerned by this. It's very curious that artists working with visually challenging and demanding problems invariably seem to favour moderation when it comes to music. Jackson Pollock may have worked to the sound of modern jazz, but in itself that was a far more commodified product still than anything he was attempting to create. Nevertheless, certain visual artists, both in the U.S.A. and U.K, seemed in relentless pursuit of a representation and form of working with paint that again underwent more rigorous change.

Talking about the move towards abstraction and paintings of flat forms with "no fictional space," Gayford states: "Hard-edge painting aimed to do away with the distinction between figure and field, subject and background,"[16] a statement that runs up against the traditions of European visual art with its figure and ground Renaissance dualism,[17] and most importantly here for us, the melody and accompaniment dualism of European-based (classical) music that formed the bedrock also for jazz, rock'n'roll, and pop musics.[18]

But the push and pull between visual art and music never held any tension or real sense of combat for me. In my teenage years music was very much uppermost in my waking hours, maybe because it was around more. My brothers, my friends, the radio, the record player, even in small-town south England, random jazz LPs would pop up in the only record-book-birthday card style shop in town, and by my mid teens I was nipping up to London to Dobells Jazz record shop to raid the downstairs second-hand department for everything I could find with Elvin Jones or Ed Blackwell playing, so long as my saved-up pocket money could stretch that far. Contemporary visual art, however, in neighbourhoods like ours was something not yet commodified, even on a small scale. That was a side to U.K. business culture yet to come, and it certainly did. Contemporary art in the U.K. has been sold—at least informationally—to the public in ways that comparative investigative/exploratory music never has. Let's not misunderstand this however: we're very far from being an informed and engaged society in relation to art or music—or maybe much else—but it's comparative... so I am told...

Even so, we can get retrospective glimmers of inter-disciplinary activity, however cerebral. George Brecht may have drawn conceptual inspiration from Pollock's drip painting—despite Pollock himself always denying that his approach involved accident—in his composition "Drip Music" (1959-1962). But what seems most interesting to me in this is not only the exchange as it were between disciplines in this Fluxus performance piece, but simply the use of water in a "musical" setting. The challenge to the assumed is what seems to matter, the "assumed" being the allowances established by tradition, habit and the media as to the conventions of instrumentation and—more importantly—how they are supposed to sound. Brecht offered a composition from a Western music perspective for water, another to add to Cage's work with both water and objects outside the conventions of "normalised" composition, and in 1966 he took the notion of performance with water a step further in the piece "For a drummer," referenced in Douglas Kahn's Noise Water Meat:

"Drum on something you have never drummed on before/Drum with something you have never drummed with before," he commands us in his Fluxus Performance Workbook, advocating the use of leaking water hoses "over a real drum splashing the leaking water all around during the performance."

JUNK

This all seems well and good, with the distinctions between sound art, foley artistry and music-making being thoroughly drowned. Not everyone's cup of tea no doubt, and for a musician with a straightforward love of playing the instrument even within the technique-stretching domains of free improvisation, this might just be something to turn off after a short while—if indeed one can.

But the point is there. Expand the creative territories, push at their boundaries.

So for me as a teenager surrounded by ideas that were already challenging conventions I knew little about, an environment of creative allowance was being established. In hindsight, the output of new American jazz, though pushing at conventions of form and vocabulary, was still maintaining the hierarchic stability of front-line/rhythm-section role-play. The commodification of sound, what a contemporary jazz group was allowed to be even in the 1960s, was somewhat entrenched. Albert Ayler's tenor saxophone blew a different tonality, as did Coltrane's tenor and soprano, as did Ornette's alto, but the essential build of the music was primarily that of the melodist/accompanist format, even if Ayler was very much challenging the rule-book. Even the free jazz groups of the later 1960s and 70s were still embodying both the instrumental and maybe thereby hierarchical conventions that had been around for 50 plus years. And if there was any percussion involved it was almost totally the Cuban conga drum or the Brazilian clave and associated ringly-dingly that fit the bill.

What should jazz have sounded like? Or even now, what can it sound like? Improvisation—as we have talked about earlier—seems to have largely been dropped from its resources. Assumptions have been maintained as to how it should all sound, what it should be doing. Financial needs have to be met. The product has to be fashioned... and the hope is that the cash registers ring.

Yet the impact of environment totalities on expression runs deeper than the simply conceptual. It's not simply style we are talking about, but those matters that underpin content. As New York art critic Clement Greenberg said to Anthony Caro in 1959, "if you want to change your art, change your habits."[19] Ways of thinking and living need to be modified, and one's relationship to the environment/planet re-examined. For a musician this seems to me, on some plateau or other, fundamental. Can music respond to and reflect what's going on, not just within an immediate context, but in how one sees the state of play nationally and internationally? And should it? The vocabularies used, the musical language, the positioning on the musical/cultural map.

On a direct interactive level, Cage had a nice comment to make on the urban situation, the correspondence between himself and the racket going on outside his window. No doubt this also related to his attitude to Muzak, feeding and filtering through to his own compositions.

I wouldn't dream of getting double glass because I love all the sounds. The traffic never stops, night and day. Every now and then a horn , siren, screeching brakes, extremely interesting and always unpredictable. At first I thought I couldn't sleep through it. Then I found a way of transposing the sounds into images so that they entered into my dreams without waking me up. A burglar alarm lasting several hours resembled a Brancusi.[20]

JUNK

In the West we can say that our understanding and perception of music is constantly being molded into genre categories announcing an acceptance of an institutionalized music industry. Offering a kind of aural de-tox, music with a freer, less rigid form, following neither the dictates of a composer nor perhaps the accepted and standardized use of an instrument (or even the use of an instrument "proper"), can open up the ability to listen to and appreciate the qualities of SOUND. Our ears have the same biological ability to listen, but as Cage indicated in his urban noise remarks, are culturally tamed and trained to recognize certain sounds as music, with the concurrent tendency to disregard the rest. And in this sense, playing music and listening to music forms a reciprocal relationship of mutual gain and pleasure, defining affordance for both the player and the listener-as-environment. Both are needed to shape the creative activities that a culture allows.

This book wants to operate within this perspective.

APPENDIX

There are quite a lot of LP's and CD's released that show my use of percussion and that might be of interest to investigate further.

Here is a very succinct sample for reference of primarily duo and trio work. In no particular order:

With Yuji Takahashi:
> *Live at Aoshima Hall* IMA-SZOK 2019 CD

With Sergio Armaroli:
> *Dance Steps* Leo Records 2021 CD

With Martin Klapper:
> *Recent Croaks* Acta Records 1997 CD

With Annette Peacock:
> *I Have No Feelings* Ironicrecords LP 1986

With Phil Minton:
> *Ammo* Leo Records LP 1984

With Witold Oleszak:
> *Fragments of Parts*
> Freeform Association 2012 CD

With John Russell:
> *Birthdays* Emanem Records 1996 CD

With Alan Silva:
  Plug In Multikulti records 2013 CD

Solo:
  Beuys's Knees White Cube/ The Vinyl Factory LP 2015

With The Croaks (Kuchen, Klapper, Turner):
  One of the Best Bears Listen!
  Foundation fs records 2018 CD

With The Recedents (Coxhill, Cooper, Turner):
  Wishing You Were Here 4 CD Box Set 1985-2008
  Freeform Association 2014

With Konk Pack (Hodgkinson, Lehn, Turner):
  Off Leash Grob Records CD 2001

Please also see: www.turners-site.com for additional discography, references and information, and YouTube for film and video documentation.

NOTES

[1] American Minimalist/Conceptual sculptor Carl Andre, 1972.

[2] H Owen Reed and Joel T Leach, *Scoring for Percussion and the Instruments of the Percussion Section*. 1969.

[3] "*Leedy Drum Topics* complete from 1923 to 1941", compiled by Rob Cook, Cedar Creek Publishing, 1993.

[4] https://fas.org/irp/doddir/army/tc1-19-30.pdf, chapter 6: suspended cymbals, striking implements.

[5] https://fas.org/irp/doddir/army/tc1-19-30.pdf, chapter 8: triangle playing area

[6] P. Tagg, "Understanding Musical Time Sense," concepts, sketches and consequences, 1984: https://www.tagg.org/articles/timesens.html

[7] There are fifty or so ways of referencing the self—"I"—in Japanese, each chosen in response to context—the where, who with, when of circumstance. The environment is crucial to self-representation. In the west, we have the single "I," unchanged by any relationship with context, should it be registered.

[8] We can all love Ornette and Coltrane and Albert Ayler—and others—and hear the closeness between lead voice and drummer gradually re-focusing, but the music still reflected the frontline instruments—the soloists—and the rhythm section hierarchy, with their positions relatively unchallenged. Cecil Taylor thankfully, did much to change all this in the world of "jazz," perhaps also realising that duos maximised democratic individual music freedom.

[9] https://www.youtube.com/watch?v=JI0NyFAd2A4 This is a great clip from a 1942 Arthur Askey film, *King Arthur Was A Gentleman*, and features in addition to Crump playing some magic on someone's spectacles and his own teeth, a very young Victor Feldman on drums, and the great Max Bacon

hamming it up, but also displaying some wonderful cymbal work. Louis Armstrong was a fan of his drumming!

[10] Hugh Pinksterboer, *The Cymbal Book*, ch. 1, "History."

[11] This is an anecdote Beecham's biographer, John Lucas, disputes, and suggests the music critic, Neville Cardus, may have been responsible for.

[12] Martin Davidson is the owner-producer of Emanem Records, a pioneering and committed company solely dedicated to the documenting of improvisation.

[13] Karl Peinkofer and Fritz Tannigel, *Handbook of Percussion Instruments*, Schott 1969 p. 156

[14] Transatlantic Re-soundings: Fats Waller's London Suite and the Jazz Atlantic by George Burrows. "In effect, the London Suite, in its transatlantic hybridity of European and African-American musical styles, upset the highly racialized critical image that had built up around Waller and his typical style of hot jazz music and entertainment." Interestingly, Burrows quotes an interview with Waller in which he states: "Throughout the British Isles and Scandinavia, audiences like to listen [...] Unlike the jitterbugs over here, they will often stop while dancing as a band builds up to the climaxes. I never saw such an intelligent appreciation of swing. [...] For years I've been trying to sell the idea of softer stuff over here but I've never been able to get away with it until now [...] I used to tell 'em down at Victor I ought to tone down, but they'd say, 'No, go ahead and give 'em that hot primitive stuff; that is what they want.' But I don't think so any more [...] I think Europe's way is the right way, and I think it'll take over here, and I hope it does before we lose our eardrums."

[15] So... I've talked myself into it. A performance piece or a workshop or even community/social function thing. Collect your instruments—plastic tubs, tin cans, bits of metal, plastic tubing, cardboard boxes, paper, knitting needles, sticks and branches, bits of wood, old doorbells, whatever your senses tell you will produce a sound you can work with. Accumulate a group of people. Sit down and play together, and make sure you are listening ! Get to where you play together for a long stretch of time, getting your ears inside what is happening. Perhaps have a piece of foam rubber on the floor in front of each of

you to act as a resonator for objects to be placed on. You could have a collection of objects in the centre that people could take from or return instruments to as the music develops. Get interested in materials, how they sound and how they look. Walk around your neighbourhood, the street markets, even your kitchen differently. Use the internet differently to source material.

[16] Martin Gayford, *Modernists & Mavericks*, Thames & Hudson, 2018, p.180.

[17] Typically putting a spanner in the works, and despite very actively embodying chance and the accident in his work, Francis Bacon—according to Frank Bowling—seemed nevertheless caught in that Renaissance web: "a stage with figures on it." (*Modernists & Mavericks*, p. 178).

[18] These are interesting pointers in our discussions of the place inside music of the form of percussion we have been talking about throughout this book. Philip Glass discusses aspects of Indian music in William Duckworth's book *Talking Music* that illustrates the division between the western alliance between harmony and melody: "The basic alliance; rhythm comes along to liven things up," he tells us, later referencing the tension between the fundamentals of melody and the rhythm in both northern and southern Indian music. Reducing the complications of harmony, this trajectory perhaps also points towards an understanding of percussion that allows its application as both rhythmic and melodic vehicles in music, combining the two. We might say that one of the great contributions to music offered by free improvisation lies in its allowance in fact of all instruments to function as both simultaneously, should they choose to be so used. It's part of the discovery process, fuelling no doubt even the breakdown of hierarchies in music making.

"Blue" Gene Tyranny, in the same book, references John Cage: "Besides knowing his music, the main thing that influenced me is just the freedom. I mean, you can really make your own music; you can just do it, you know."

[19] Quoted in *Modernists & Mavericks*, p. 288.

[20]Stephen Montague: "John Cage at Seventy," *American Music*, vol. 3, no. 2, 1985, p. 205.

Roger Turner has been working as an improvising drummer-percussionist since the early 1970's, collaborating in numerous international established and ad hoc configurations. He remains one of those players who have collectively redefined the language of contemporary percussion.

Solo work, intense acoustic duo collaborations, work with electro-acoustic ensembles & open-form song, extensive work with dance and visual artists, plus specific jazz-based ensembles have brought collaborations with many of the most interesting European & international musicians and performers, including Annette Peacock, Phil Minton, Charles Gayle, Lol Coxhill, Derek Bailey, Otomo Yoshihide, Alan Silva, Keith Rowe, Cecil Taylor, Yuji Takahashi, Josef Nadj, Min Tanaka, Toshinori Kondo, Roy Campbell, etc., etc.

He has toured and played concerts worldwide from Sydney to the Arctic, Tokyo to Belfast, New York to Beirut, Sao Paulo to Auckland.

www.turners-site.com
en.wikipedia.org/
wiki/Roger_Turner_(musician)

Born in Tokyo, **Mari Kamada** comes from a classically-trained musical family. She studied piano and composition for 12 years before working in commercial film production for the advertising company Hakuhodo. She then worked alongside the renowned art curator Junji Ito and later continued as both a freelance media organizer and an art coordinator.

Mari moved to London, U.K. in 1999 to pursue an intensive period of academic research into Japanese socio-cultural phenomena at Goldsmiths.

She currently researches an extremely wide spectrum of U.K. life for all the major Japanese TV companies and writes articles on ecological psychology and social tropes specific to Japan, as well as on the visual arts of both Japan and the West. Mari is preparing a book on sublime dreams.

Made in the USA
Middletown, DE
30 October 2022

13746379R00104